RESOURCE KIT

IIADE FOR MORE

SIX ESSENTIAL SHIFTS FOR CREATING A CULTURE OF MOBILIZATION

PARTICIPANT'S GUIDE

CREATED BY
TODD WILSON & ROB WEGNER

**SMALL GROUP STUDY FOR CHURCH LEADERS
THROUGH THE BOOK OF EPHESIANS**

Exponential is a growing movement of activists committed to the multiplication of healthy new churches. Exponential Resources spotlights actionable principles, ideas and solutions for the accelerated multiplication of healthy, reproducing faith communities. For more information, visit exponential.org.

The vision of Multipliers is to see every Christian mobilized into their unique, God-given purpose and for healthy Biblical mobilization to become a normative measure of success in the church. We are passionate about seeing a movement of everyday Christians mobilized into their unique personal callings in the mission fields where they work, live, study and play. Find out more at www.multipliers.org.

ISBN-13: 978-1-62424-015-7
Edited by Jenna Smith - StoryLabs (storylabs.info)
Layout by Don Smith/Josh Lazar - StoryLabs (storylabs.info)
and by Karen Pheasant
Cover Design by - Ox Creative/StoryLabs

MADE FOR MORE

SPECIAL THANKS

Special thanks to the amazing leaders that took the time to record the videos that are a part of the resource kit:

Alan Hirsch	Dave Ferguson	Danielle Strickland
Michael Frost	John Mark Comer	Craig Terndrup
Noemi Chavez	D.A. Horton	Léonce Crump
Brian Sanders	Drew Hyun	Jeff Vanderstelt
Sam Stephens	Randy Frazee	Brian Phipps

We also want to thank the churches that were involved in the case studies for this resource kit:

Gateway Church
Craig Terndrup, and Eric Snodgrass.

The Underground
Brian Sanders

Soma Family of Churches
Jeff Vanderstelt

Bridgetown Church
John Mark Comer

Austin Stone Church
Scott Hekman, Lydia Hekman

Westside Family Church
Andy Traub, Brian Johnson, and Brian Phipps

We would also like to thank Don Smith, Jenna Smith and the rest of the team at StoryLabs (storylabs.info) and Karen Pheasant for their amazing job with editing and formatting this resource kit.

≡XPONENTIAL⌐

MARCH 4-7, 2019
ORLANDO, FL

TOUR CITIES

WASHINGTON, D.C.
SOUTHERN, CA
BAY AREA, CA
HOUSTON, TX
CHICAGO, IL
NEW YORK, NY

IIIADE FOR MOR≡

SPEAKERS

J.D. GREEAR | OYSTEIN GJERME | ALBERT TATE
DAVE FERGUSON | CYNTHIA MARSHALL | ALAN HIRSCH
DREW HYUN | DAVE CLAYTON | + MORE

FEATURING: TONY DUNGY | LECRAE | + MORE

J.D. GREEAR   CYNTHIA MARSHALL   ALAN HIRSCH   ALBERT TATE

SPECIAL INVITATION
MADE FOR MORE EVENTS

The 2019 Exponential Theme is Made for More: Mobilizing God's People, God's Way. Join us at one of our seven Made for More events starting with our national event in Orlando, Florida. Additional regional events provide opportunities to bring your entire team to an event closer to home.

This book is a taste of our 2019 Made for More theme. Please consider attending one of our seven Exponential 2019 events. Our goal is to help shape your paradigm for multiplication, inspire and encourage you to multiply, and equip you to turn ideas into action. Our 2019 conferences are built on the content of this book and are designed to help you move from ideas and inspiration to implementation and impact.

2019 THEME
MADE FOR MORE:
MOBILIZING GOD'S PEOPLE, GOD'S WAY

2019 NATIONAL MADE FOR MORE EVENT
Exponential // Orlando, Florida // March 4 – 7, 2019

Our national conference, Exponential, is a full-service event in Orlando, Florida with thousands of attendees, 150+ speakers, 40 tracks, 200 workshops and 12+ pre-conference equipping labs.

2019 REGIONAL HEROMAKER EVENTS
Washington DC, Southern CA, Northern CA, Chicago IL, Houston TX, and New York City, NY

Our Exponential regional events are shorter and geographically based which translates to lower overall costs for large teams. Regionals bring the full "punch" of the national conferences' five main stage sessions without the breakout workshops.

www.exponential.org/events

FIND YOUR PLACE:

LOCATING YOUR CALLING THROUGH GIFTS, PASSIONS AND STORY

The G.P.S. personal calling discovery and deployment featured in this book will be available through the next book in the Exponential series, *Find Your Place: Locating Your Calling Through Gifts, Passions and Story* by Rob Wegner and Brian Phipps.

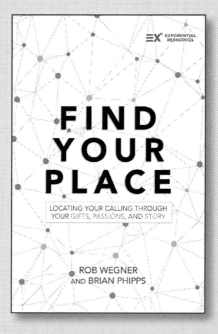

COMING MARCH 2019

Releasing at The Exponential Conference in Orlando, Florida.

INSIDE

MADE FOR MORE
INTRODUCTION

2019

VIDEOS CAN BE ACCESSED AT
EXPONENTIAL.ORG/MORE

INTRODUCTION

The church in the U.S. is the largest and most effective volunteer mobilizer on the planet!

What other organization mobilizes as many people on a daily basis for service? Can you think of just one other organization that even comes close? In fact, if you could add up the next ten largest national organizations that mobilize volunteers, the combined totals would likely pale in comparison to the overall number of volunteers and enlisted hours the local church mobilizes on a weekly basis.

Now, assign a minimum hourly wage rate to those hours, and the church in the U.S. becomes one of the largest economies in the world!

Over the years, many churches have made the shift to gift-based volunteerism. What a big difference that has made. What an important and necessary step forward. So many more people are now serving the programs of the local church in ways that are more fruitful and fulfilling.

Amidst this seemingly prosperous church economy, we are now seeing a surge in churches who are embracing and implementing internal leadership development programs (or pipelines) to help scale the mobilization of volunteers and grow the programs of the church.

Go God! Go God's people!

But, to what end and for what purpose are we doing this? If you're reading this resource, you're probably carrying a discontentedness.

We get it. We've carried the same sense that something just isn't right.

INTRODUCTION
MADE FOR MORE ▶

Yet, amidst all the success, we knew and continue to understand there's something about this entire system of mobilization that feels off. We bet you feel it too.

This tension lurks uncomfortably in the background, waiting faithfully for another Sunday to arrive so we can start the process all over again. And, Sundays always come! Each week, you've got dozens if not hundreds of volunteer "slots" that need to be filled to bring the ministry programs of the church alive.

Let's be honest. This can feel disheartening and add to our sense that something is wrong.

If we aren't careful, we experience one of two extremes. Either, we burn out of ministry from its heavy demands, or we slip into a utilitarian approach to mobilization. This is where we see people as a consumable commodity, a means to an end to make our programs run. We admit there have been times when we've instinctively taken this low road. For many of us, it's as if volunteer mobilization is a foundational, physiological and safety need in Maslow's hierarchy of basic personal needs.

THE ACRONYM THAT BEST DESCRIBES OUR MOBILIZATION APPROACH IN THESE MOMENTS OF DESPAIR IS "N.A.G."

NEED... TO FILL - "I need to fill this slot before Sunday!"
ACCOST... A MEMBER - "I need you to do this for Jesus!"
GUILT... USED LIBERALLY - "If you don't, lost people will go to hell!"

Deep down, you know there's a better way, but your current paradigm is holding you captive. Your approach is not optimized to mobilize God's people, God's way!

You've had conversations with devoted volunteers who've checked all the boxes for engagement with your programs. In spite of this, they're also experiencing an underlying uneasiness that is whispering, "There must be something more."

INTRODUCTION ▶
MADE FOR MORE

Together, your discontent and the unease of those you lead, screams out that the church and its people are designed and Made for More. So much more!The pent-up, latent capacity of Christians who've never discovered and engaged their unique purpose on earth represents an unstoppable movement for good. As leaders, it's our responsibility to steward this amazing opportunity! We can experience the blessings of seeing the untapped potential of God's people transformed into active energy.

It's been said that insanity is doing the same things over and over again but hoping for different outcomes. You want to see the latent capacity of God's people released, but you are not sure how to break out of the paradigms and processes that bind you to your past ways.

Good news! Exponential's theme throughout all of 2019 is "Made for More: Mobilizing God's People, God's Way!" We've developed this new resource kit specifically for church staff, elders and teams to be a catalyst for shifting your paradigm and helping you break free from unhealthy mobilization cultures.

You may be wondering, "What is this new way of mobilizing God's people?" It's not actually new. Rather, it is the ancient method of the early church that began a movement and turned the Roman Empire upside down, transforming culture and history as we know it.

Helping you rediscover this forgotten but essential approach for mobilizing God's pople, God's way is our motivation for developing this kit.

THE UNDERLYING METAPHOR

You're probably familiar with Home Depot's slogan, "You can do it. We can help." In so doing, Home Depot positions themselves as the resource and training center for millions. The message is clear, "We are here to help YOU accomplish your unique project." That is the essence of this new, but ancient, approach to mobilizing God's people, God's way.

Too often the church functions with a 'we can do it, you can help' approach. Imagine a church that functions with a 'you can do it, how can we help' approach!

INTRODUCTION
MADE FOR MORE

At first, this may seem completely unmanageable and highly chaotic. Ministry leaders often say, "So you're saying, people just come up with projects; and then, we're supposed to fund and execute those?" Or, "Now we'll have dozens or hundreds of new ministries, basically one for every member to promote and recruit to?" Or, "Everyone just abandons the current programs and starts new 501c3s or something?"

Nope, that's not what we're talking about. Let's clarify what the "we can do it" versus "you can do it" approach looks like in the church.

"*WE* CAN DO IT. *YOU* CAN HELP."

PROGRAM-FOCUSED
Most ministry happens in the programs of the organized church.

VOLUNTEER-CENTRIC
The programs have mostly predetermined slots that need to be filled by volunteers.

INTERNALLY-DRIVEN
Operating the internal programs of the church, including Sunday mornings, consumes 90% or more of volunteer hours. This approach fails to tap into the abundant capacity of the collective of God's people, each equipped with a unique sweet spot of personal calling.

VS.

"*YOU* CAN DO IT. *WE* CAN HELP."

"ALL OF LIFE"-FOCUSED
Most ministry happens where we live, work, study and play.

CALLING-CENTRIC
Ministry includes all of your life. Everyone has a unique sweet spot of calling that integrates his or her gifts, passions, burdens and God-ordained life experiences.

EXTERNALLY-DRIVEN
Mobilization is as much about sending as it is about attracting and accumulating.

INTRODUCTION ▸
MADE FOR MORE

The role of the local church, in this approach, is to be the mobilizing home base. This empowers all disciples to discover their personal calling and then deploy them to express the fullness of Jesus into every corner of culture and into every sphere of society.

THE UNDERLYING GOAL

This study aims to help churches move from an operating system characterized by "We can do it. You can help." to a new way of thinking characterized by "You can do it. We can help." This transformation in thinking will help you refocus your mobilization strategies. It will position you to find better balance between attracting and accumulating volunteers AND developing and releasing everyday missionaries into VS everyday mission fields where people live, work and play.

Understand, this is not about throwing out all that is good with your current approach in search of an elusive silver bullet. It's important to steward and build on the islands of health and strength in which God has blessed you. However, this study will challenge you to rethink your paradigm and consider whether a system reset is needed in your context.

You must discern between revolutionary change OR evolutionary change in your context. Can you simply evolve beyond where you are now to where you need to be, OR do you need a system reset? Are the strategies and behaviors that got you where you are today the same ones that can help you achieve a more balanced approach to the "come and see" and "go and be" priorities of mobilizing God's people, God's way?

Our prayer is that this study and the shared experience with your team will be a pivotal milestone or fork in the road in the life of your church. We hope it will guide you through answering some tough questions together and discerning a path forward to a new season and chapter in your church's life.

"WE FEEL YOUR DISCONTENT"

Todd Wilson...

Before being called into full-time vocational ministry, I was a nuclear engineer for fifteen years. After leaving my secular career, I served for six years as an executive pastor at New Life Christian Church, a multisite, externally focused, aggressive church planting church in the Washington, D.C. area. Currently, New Life's leadership sends me as an entrepreneurial missionary to promote church planting and multiplication where I get to focus on new initiatives that seek to see multiplication become a normative measure of success in churches throughout the U.S.

I'm passionate about the local church AND about personal calling and seeing the release of the latent capacity embedded in the pews of the U.S. church. I spent five years writing *More: Find Your Personal Calling and Live Life to the Fullest Measure*. In my role as CEO of Exponential, I have the blessing of a front-row seat in serving thousands of networks, denominations and local churches.

Rob Wegner...

I'm currently a teaching pastor at a large church in Kansas City, Westside Family Church, where I also oversee all of our global efforts in church planting and orphan care. Furthermore, I help equip our people to live on mission in their neighborhoods in Kansas City through the development of micro-churches.

Prior to that, I wore many hats: youth, young adults, discipleship, missions, worship and the arts, chair set up expert for mobile church, etc. This was during a 22-year journey with a church plant that started in a movie theater and living rooms and became one of the fastest growing and most influential churches in America through the 1990's and 2000's, Granger Community Church near South Bend, Indiana.

In other words, we've walked a lot of miles in your shoes. We get the grind. We get the challenges of running the programs of the church. We've experienced powerful impact within the prevailing model of mobilization.

INTRODUCTION
MADE FOR MORE

Paul's letter to the churches in Ephesus provides our roadmap. We will work through each of the six chapters together. Each chapter highlights a theme element, a critical move, and an essential shift in thinking and behavior to put us on a pathway toward mobilizing God's people, God's way.

THEME ELEMENTS
- EPHESIANS 1   MADE FOR MORE
- EPHESIANS 2   MADE TO BE MORE
- EPHESIANS 3   MADE TO LOVE MORE
- EPHESIANS 4   MADE TO DO MORE
- EPHESIANS 5   MADE TO GO MORE
- EPHESIANS 6   MADE TO WIN MORE

CRITICAL MOVES
- EPHESIANS 1   MYSTERIES: ILLUMINATE THE MYSTERY
- EPHESIANS 2   MASTERPIECES: INVESTIGATE THE DESIGN
- EPHESIANS 3   MOTIVATIONS: MOTIVATE WITH LOVE
- EPHESIANS 4   MISSIONARIES: ORGANIZE FOR FULLNESS
- EPHESIANS 5   MISSION FIELDS: ACTIVATE WITH PURPOSE
- EPHESIANS 6   METHODS: PREPARE FOR BATTLE

ESSENTIAL SHIFTS
- EPHESIANS 1   FROM MORE EFFORT ... TO MORE JESUS
- EPHESIANS 2   FROM MORE VOLUNTEERS ... TO MORE MASTERPIECES
- EPHESIANS 3   FROM MORE GUILT ... TO MORE LOVE
- EPHESIANS 4   FROM MORE HIERARCHY ... TO MORE MISSIONARIES
- EPHESIANS 5   FROM MORE PROGRAMS ... TO MORE MISSION FIELDS
- EPHESIANS 6   FROM MORE STRATEGY ... TO MORE SURRENDER

INTRODUCTION ▶
MADE FOR MORE

THE INVESTMENT

Your investment? This investment as a team will sow the seeds for a change in your church's culture and the trajectory of your impact. The resource kit is FREE and easily customizable to your unique context. We encourage you to schedule this 7-week study to run as a small group with your team, and if possible, your elders and other key leaders. A church-wide campaign, which includes a sermon series and small group kit, will also be available in 2019.

THE JOURNEY

How does the study work? This entails a combination of pre-meeting preparation by participants and a dynamic, interactive weekly team meeting. The kit is also designed for each staff member, elder and team leader to use the study with their groups. In this way, all the leaders of the church can be aligned on the same paradigm-shifting content so that they can help others own the vision within their unique context.

1. Individual Preparation (Individual Time: 75 minutes/week)

Each week before the group discussion, participants should:

a. Read the lesson from the Made for More study. (15 minutes)

b. Read the corresponding chapter from Ephesians. (5 minutes)

c. Watch one or two videos. (30 minutes). The first video is focused on teaching content from Ephesians and the accompanying shift. The second video is a case study of a local church that has embodied that shift with solid results.

d. Answer personal reflection and assessment questions. (10 minutes)

e. Read the description of the week's required shift, and reflect on where your church stands on making the shift. (5 minutes)

MADE FOR MORE

2. Group Discussion for Seven Weeks covering the Six Moves and an Action Plan (Group Time: 90 minutes/week)

Each week, you will gather with your team for an interactive conversation about one chapter from the book of Ephesians. With each chapter of Ephesians, we will highlight one theme element, one critical move and one essential shift (all listed above). You will maintain an ongoing list of team "aha" moments, significant learnings, conclusions and potential changes.

The aggregation and integration of these elements create the context for an operating system that mobilizes God's people, God's way. After working through the six chapters of Ephesians, the closing lesson *(Lesson 7)* focuses on developing a prioritized list of next step actions for your team. This list of WINS (What's important now) will help your team rally around and take ownership for moving the church forward based on your discoveries in the first six lessons.

AGENDA FOR WEEKLY MEETINGS

- A Short Introduction of the Theme — 5 minutes
- Discussion Questions on the Pre-Meeting Content — 10 minutes
- Watch Teaching Video located at **exponential.org/more** — 15 - 25 minutes
- Paradigm Conversation and Discussion Questions — 10 minutes
- Perspective and Assessment Conversations — 20 minutes
- Key Shift and Potential Changes Conversation — 15 minutes
- Prayer — 5 minutes

NOTE: Lesson 7 is a planning lesson for prioritizing "What's Important Now" (WINS) and starting the process of putting an action plan in place. This lesson will take more time and may need to be one extended three-hour lesson or several shorter lessions.

WEEKEND RETREAT OPTION: You might choose a retreat format/ environment for team members and their spouses for the final planning lesson.

MADE FOR MORE
LESSON 01

2019

VIDEOS CAN BE ACCESSED AT
EXPONENTIAL.ORG/MORE

MADE FOR MORE

SCRIPTURE: EPHESIANS 1

Key Verses: Ephesians 1:22-23
And God placed all things under his feet and appointed him to be head over everything for the church, which is his body, the fullness of him who fills everything in every way.

MOVE #1: ILLUMINATE THE MYSTERY

SHIFT #1: FROM MORE EFFORT... TO MORE JESUS

BIG IDEA: JESUS IS MORE.

Only Jesus can fill everything in every way. A core commitment of every local church is to continually illuminate this mystery: Jesus is More. Therefore, the Church is made for More. The Church is chosen by Jesus to express His fullness into every corner of culture and into every sphere of society.

Pathway: This lesson consists of approximately one hour of advance preparation work for team members and a 75 to 90 minute interactive group gathering.

LESSON 01
MADE FOR MORE ▶

- Read Ephesians 1and answer reflection questions. (10 minutes)

- Watch Video #1 – Rob Wegner on Ephesians 1 (15 minutes) and fill in the answers below.

- Watch Video #2 – Case Study of Soma Communities (10 minutes) and write down at least one observation that captured your thinking.

- Read Lesson 1 and complete the discussion questions. (25 minutes)

  - Reflect on the Introduction and answer the Discussion Questions.

  - Complete the questions in the church, team, and personal assessment sections. These questions will be used for rich conversations among team members during the team gathering. Be sure to invest time working through these assessment questions.

- Prayer – Spend some time praying that God will reveal needed changes in you, your team, your church and that your team will be unified on a path forward.

TEAM GATHERING

• Read Ephesians 1 together	5 minutes
• Discuss Introduction questions	10 minutes
• Watch Video #3 together – Michael Frost	25 minutes
• Discuss Video #3 and Key Paradigm Thoughts	10 minutes
• Team Perspective and Assessment – Discuss assessment questions	20 minutes
• Shift #1 discussion and action	15 minutes
• Preview Lesson 2 expectations and prayer	5 minutes

INDIVIDUAL
PREPARATION

1. Read Ephesians 1. Pretend you've never experienced church and that what you read in Ephesians 1 is your first and only exposure to church. What conclusions or assumptions would you make about church?

2. Ephesians 1:22-23 tells us the church is a representation of Jesus's body that can fill everything in every way. What practical examples can you think of in life where one thing can completely fill another thing? List at least 1-2 things.

3. What does the truth of Ephesians 1:22-23 say about the church's potential for reaching into every nook and cranny of society with the fullness of Jesus?

   Although it's implied, the verses don't tell us how we are to carry Jesus's fullness into all corners of society. If we were being obedient to and taking full advantage of the mystery of Jesus' fullness in us and through us to mobilize God's people, God's way, what would that look like? How would we do it?

   How would this mobilization approach differ from the strategies we currently use to recruit volunteers?

4. What, in particular, about the passage convicted you personally about something in your life and leadership?

LESSON 01
MADE FOR MORE

The book of Ephesians gives solid, biblical insights for mobilizing God's people, God's way. Why?

Reason 1: The book of Ephesians is _____.

Reason 2: The book of Ephesians is _____.

Ephesians 1 begins with a _____ of praise for the

Christ and ends with a _____ prayer for the Church.

Ephesians 1:1-14: A _____ of praise for the Christ.

In other words, "**Jesus is** _____!"

Ephesians 1:15-22: A _____ prayer for the Church.

In other words, "**The Church is** _____ **for More!**"

Ephesians 1:22-23
And God <u>placed all things under his feet</u> and appointed him to be head over everything for the church, which is his body, the fullness of him who fills everything in every way.

As church leaders our first concern is this: We would be obsessed with

Jesus ever growing _____ in our minds and in our

hearts.

ꟽADE FOR MORⱻ _____

LESSON 01
INDIVIDUAL PREP

MOVE #1

Illuminate the _____ of MORE!

Ephesians 1:22-23
And God placed all things under his feet and appointed him to be head over everything for the church, which is his body, the fullness of him who fills everything in every way.

The church is not a building; it's a _____.

The church is not an activity; it's an _____.

The church is not a program; it's the people of God saved by the power of God for the purposes of God.

The church is all the people of God on an everyday mission to fill

everything, everywhere with the _____.

Paul's Christology shapes his _____.

> **CHRISTOLOGY:**
> The branch of theology relating to the person, nature and role of Jesus Christ.
>
> **ECCLESIOLOGY:**
> The branch of theology as applied to the nature and structure of the Church.

LESSON 01
MADE FOR MORE ▶

What does it mean for us to be the fullness of Jesus?

We are the primary means to _____ Jesus' presence?

CASE STUDY OF SOMA COMMUNITIES   *7 MINUTES*
WATCH VIDEO #2

In this video, you'll get to see how Soma Communities is applying Move #1, Illuminating the Mystery of More.

OBSERVATIONS:
Highlight at least one observation that really grabbed your attention from the video.

READ LESSON 1, REFLECT AND PRAY   *25 MINUTES*

Review the Lesson 1 content from the past few pages (The Key Verses, the Move, the Shift, the Big Idea, your Notes from Ephesians and the Teaching Video Notes) and complete the following:

1. What stood out to you from the Lesson 1 reading material and videos? Why?

2. Flip forward to the Conversation Guide section, and review the questions in the **church and team assessment** inside the lesson. These questions will be used for deeper conversations among team members during the team gathering. Be sure to invest time reflecting on these assessment questions.

3. The theme of this lesson is "Made for More: Illuminate the Mystery." What is the "mystery"? Why is it vital for us to "illuminate" this mystery as our first move?

4. Our first shift is "From More Effort … to More Jesus." How would you instinctively characterize this shift in your own words from your own experience?

What is your biggest fear in pursuing this shift?

What keeps you from seeing every Christ-follower as an everyday missionary with a unique mission field for illuminating the fullness and mystery of Jesus where they live, work and play?

5. Personal Reflection: How well am I doing at revealing the fullness of Jesus where I live, work, study and play?

6. Spend some time praying that God will reveal needed changes in you, your team, your church and that your team will be unified on a path forward.

CONVERSATION
GUIDE

LESSON 01
MADE FOR MORE

In this lesson, we jump into Ephesians 1.

Ephesians 1:22-23
"And God placed all things under his feet and appointed him to be head over everything for the church, which is his body, the fullness of him who fills everything in every way."

MOVE #1: ILLUMINATE THE MYSTERY

SHIFT #1: FROM MORE EFFORT ... TO MORE JESUS

BIG IDEA: JESUS IS MORE.

Only Jesus can fill everything in every way. A core commitment of every local church is to continually illuminate this mystery: Jesus is More. Therefore, the Church is Made for More. The Church is chosen by Jesus to express His fullness into every corner of culture and into every sphere of society.

The discussions in this study will be rich and fruitful. Stay mindful of the time as each question only has 3 to 4 minutes allotted. Fully engage the interaction with your team, but be careful not to dominate the conversation. Seek first to listen, allowing others the opportunity to share their thoughts. Let your thinking be stimulated, but don't feel like the tension in every question needs to be relieved.

DISCUSSION QUESTIONS

1. Read Ephesians 1 together. How would you describe the mystery embedded in Ephesians 1:22-23?

2. What does it mean for the church to be the fullness of Jesus in everything and every way?

3. What are the implications for how the church mobilizes God's people?

4. What stood out to you from the Lesson 1 reading, reflection questions and videos? Why?

MICHAEL FROST - MADE FOR MORE   *20 MINUTES*
WATCH VIDEO #3 TOGETHER AS A TEAM

RETHINKING OUR PARADIGM   *15 MINUTES*
ILLUMINATING THE MYSTERY OF MORE

A paradigm is what you think before you think about it. You'll never experience lasting change without examining those thoughts and allowing the Word and the Spirit to transform your assumptions.

Let's assume for this conversation that some aspects of your team and church paradigm for mobilization are wrong. Not necessarily all aspects may be wrong but at least some. Let's assume that these gaps are limiting your ability to mobilize God's people, God's way. Let's have an honest and open conversation to discover where there might be faults in your paradigm of mobilization.

Here are some key paradigm shifting ideas from Michael Frost's talk. Read through these as a team. Read through the Key Paradigm Thoughts below as a team. Then, spend time talking through the Discussion Questions as a team.

KEY PARADIGM THOUGHT

If the *incarnational mission* of Jesus reminds us that we are the sent ones, the resurrectional mission of Jesus reminds us that we are the *mobilizing ones*. We believe every nook and cranny of the whole world is under the authority of our magnificent, cosmic King Jesus. WE are mobilized to fill everything everywhere with the fullness of Jesus. The resurrected Christ reminds us there is no place where we are not sent!

KEY PARADIGM THOUGHT

Paul says, "Be discrete," when it comes to meat offered to idols. But, he refuses steadfastly to say, "Do not eat the meat offered to an idol." He knows if he were to say, "Don't ever eat it," the prohibition would completely isolate believers from society. The social dislocation from culture that Paul anticipated as crushing the Christian movement, Frost contends, is the very place where many churches and Christians are today. The resurrected Christ, on the other hand, is calling us to go everywhere! We join Him in what He is doing in those places.

LESSON 01
CONVERSATION GUIDE ▶

KEY PARADIGM THOUGHT

In the incarnation, a piece of Heaven came to Earth. In the ascension, a piece of Earth went into Heaven. With this dual action in Jesus, the Kingdom of God is at hand. Heaven and Earth are colliding and commingling in His Kingdom. Where wouldn't we go to join Jesus? Who wouldn't we mobilize? Christ is already everywhere, even the darkest corners of the world.

KEY PARADIGM THOUGHT

God doesn't want our pre-existing laundry list of all we will do for Him. Jesus wants our blank sheet of paper and for us to say, "Write anything."

DISCUSSION QUESTIONS FROM THE MICHAEL FROST VIDEO

1. What challenged and confronted you the most?

2. What encouraged and comforted you the most?

3. What tensions are you feeling? Why?

LESSON 01
MADE FOR MORE

TEAM NOTES
Have someone on your team create an "official set of notes" with your answers to the questions in this section and in the subsequent "Shift Section." Make it comprehensive and inclusive of the collective representation of your team. Seek to get as much unity of perspective as possible on your conclusions. Email the updated list to the team after each team meeting. Each week, add your new notes to the end of the previous week's notes so that by Lesson 7, you have a comprehensive set of assessment and perspective notes for use in developing an action plan.

UNDERSTANDING OUR PARADIGM
Paradigm shifts are deeper and harder work than you might initially think. Before you can ascend to a new paradigm, you must first descend from the safety of your current paradigm. You must travel through the valley that separates your old thinking from your new thinking. If you try to leap from peak to peak (paradigm to paradigm) without traveling through the valley, you will likely remain stuck in the safety of your current paradigm.

This journey through the valley is often confusing, chaotic and challenging. It may feel like bullets are flying at you from unexpected directions, and you will be tempted to retreat back to the safety of the current paradigm. It's similar to the journey of the Israelites out of Egypt. The challenges directly in their path clouded and prevented them from seeing the beautiful and fertile land that awaited them. Many of those people felt it better to retreat to the captivity of their past rather than face the challenges that would lie ahead of them. It took courage and the surrender to God's leading to move forward.

Paradigm shifts require that you look at your current context in a new way. You must confront your fears and the deep-rooted factors that hold you captive to your current ways of thinking.

In each part of the following team conversation, you are asked to look at your context but in a new way. Although two approaches will be presented as contrasts, we fully acknowledge and celebrate the need for both! However, we're asking you to consider: "Do you embrace both approaches? Is it balanced? Are we biased to one approach?" We've purposely created the contrast to help you see the same picture in a new way. We hope it's not perceived as an attack but an opportunity to stretch.

IIIADE FOR MORE

LESSON 01
CONVERSATION GUIDE ▶

CHURCH ASSESSMENT

Remember, right now you are making a thoughtful, grace-filled and brutally honest assessment of your church, your team and your lives. You'll collect thoughts on how to apply this along the way, but you won't make any decision on your future direction until your final lesson.

It is important for your team to assess and gain perspective on where you are, where you've been and where you are headed in your current paradigm. Along the way, you need to allow the Holy Spirit to reveal new perspectives and needed shifts in your future paradigm for mobilization.

1. Let's go back to our Home Depot analogy from the Introduction. Take a minute and place a check mark next to each of the six statements below that apply to your church.

THE "WE CAN BUILD IT. YOU CAN HELP." APPROACH TO ILLUMINATING THE MYSTERY OF MORE

☐ We illuminate the fullness of Jesus in our worship services. You can volunteer to help us or attend a service.

☐ We deepen your understanding of Jesus and proclaim the Gospel by providing great teachers and curriculum. You can come receive this wonderful teaching and bring a friend.

☐ The primary place to Illuminate the Mystery of More is at the building through programs and events. The bias of our church is "Come and do!"

THE "YOU CAN BUILD IT. WE CAN HELP." APPROACH TO ILLUMINATING THE MYSTERY OF MORE

☐ We will equip you, as a disciple of Jesus, to illuminate the fullness of Jesus in a lifestyle of worship and mission where you live, work, study and play.

☐ We will equip you to live in the Lordship of Jesus by gospeling yourself daily in every area of your life. By so doing, you will be ready to gospel others where they live, work, study and play.

☐ The primary place to Illuminate the Mystery of More is in every corner of culture and every sphere of society by mobilizing all the people of God to reveal the fullness of Jesus there. The direction of our church is "Go and be!"

2. Which ones did you check? Unpack why.

3. How balanced are you between the two approaches?

Which ones are you biased toward?

4. What is the primary message being perceived by people in your church?

5. If you had to guess, what percentage of your congregation sees the church as a living body and not as a building? What percentage of your congregation sees the church as the people of God called to fill EVERYWHERE EVERY WAY with the fullness of Jesus?

6. How "obsessed" are you, as a church, with Jesus growing ever-larger in your minds and in your hearts?

7. How are you doing at equipping every disciple to grow in the Lordship of Jesus, to grow in their ability to Gospel themselves and to be able to share the gospel where they live, work, study and play?

8. The Soma Communities Case Study provided an example of how one movement is working out the "You Can Build It. We Can Help" approach. What were your impressions as you watched the Case Study of Soma Communities?

LESSON 01
MADE FOR MORE ▶

TEAM ASSESSMENT

1. How would you rate your commitment as a team to the "You Can Build It. We Can Help." approach of Illuminating the Mystery of More?

2. As a team, how united are you around Paul's vision for the church being the Body of Christ, filling everything in every way with the fullness of Jesus?

PURSUING THE SHIFT: *15 MINUTES*
FROM MORE EFFORT ... TO MORE JESUS

TEAM NOTES
Add your team's conclusions in this section into the master list highlighted in the previous section. By capturing this perspective now, you will have what's needed to develop a solid action plan in Lesson 7.

The "Shift" section is intended to build on the previous Team Perspective section and help you start the process of moving from good ideas and intentions about illuminating the mystery of the fullness of Jesus into tangible action.

These six essential shifts collectively integrate to create a culture of Mobilization God's Way. In each of the six core lessons, you are looking at one shift to discern (1) where you are as a church today, (2) what mobilization in your church could look like in five years if you fully embraced the shift and (3) specific issues that would need to be addressed to make the shift successful.

In this lesson, you are focused on the shift:
FROM MORE EFFORT ... TO MORE JESUS!

The following exercise and questions are not intended to finalize your actions, but it is instead meant to get you thinking toward the future and unified on some core conclusions and convictions. You will be working through the six shifts leading up to your final lesson *(Lesson 7)* where you will seek to integrate what you've learned into a priority list of actions to investigate and pursue. For now, don't be limited by what you think you can and cannot do. Rather, dream about a future in which this shift becomes a reality.

IIIADE FOR MOR≡

LESSON 01
CONVERSATION GUIDE ▶

DISCUSSION QUESTIONS:

1. Read through the following distinctions between **more effort** and **more Jesus**. Assess where you are as a church on the spectrum of "more effort" versus "more Jesus".

MORE EFFORT MEANS...

☐ We illuminate the fullness of Jesus in our worship services. You can volunteer to help us or attend a service.Merely human effort producing merely human result.

☐ We illuminate the fullness of Jesus in our worship services. You can volunteer to help us or attend a service.An over dependence upon human charisma, human stamina, human ingenuity and titles/rank.

☐ We illuminate the fullness of Jesus in our worship services. You can volunteer to help us or attend a service.Perfunctory prayer at the beginning or end of the meeting.

☐ We illuminate the fullness of Jesus in our worship services. You can volunteer to help us or attend a service. The gospel is shared "occasionally" with an altar call on the weekend.

☐ We illuminate the fullness of Jesus in our worship services. You can volunteer to help us or attend a service.Mobilization is striving to find enough volunteers to fill the service slots to keep things running.

MORE JESUS MEANS...

☐ To start by working from a place of rest in the gospel and identity in Christ.

☐ To practice a radical dependence on the Spirit. We begin from a place of deep listening and response to the Spirit of God within us and among us. We long to be Spirit-led and Spirit-empowered. Naturally supernatural is the new normal.

☐ To pray without ceasing. We only go forward as fast as we can on our knees.

☐ The gospel is shared every day, first with ourselves, and then, with others.

☐ Mobilization is helping people discover their unique calling and equipping them as everyday missionaries where they live, work and play.

2. Is this a shift that is worth the effort to pursue and to see put in place? How important is it to you? Why or why not?

3. In five years from now, if you were mobilizing God's people, God's way with an approach that was rooted in "more Jesus" rather than "more effort," what would that look like? What would the characteristics of success be? What benefits? Create a list of characteristics that collectively describes a preferable future.

4. What challenges and obstacles would you face? What specific issues do you know would need to be addressed? Are there actions you already know you'd need to take that can be identified now? Are there any that you suspect are needed but require more investigation? Highlight them in your list.

AT THIS POINT, YOU'RE JUST COLLECTING IDEAS.
YOU SHOULDN'T MAKE ANY DECISIONS UNTIL LESSON 7.

NEXT WEEK

Next week, we move on to Ephesians 2, Move #2 and Essential Shift #2. Be sure that you have the Participant's Guide for Lesson 2 and that you understand what work is to be completed before the next gathering.

• Read Ephesians 2 and Lesson 2. Journal your observations.

• Watch Video #4 (Rob Wegner on Ephesians 2).

• Watch Video #5 (Case Study of Westside Family Church).

CLOSING PRAYER

IIIADE FOR MOR≡

MADE FOR MORE

LESSON 02

2019

MADE TO BE MORE

SCRIPTURE: EPHESIANS 2

Ephesians 2:8-10
"For it is by grace you have been saved, through faith - and this is not from yourselves, it is the gift of God - not by works, so that no one can boast. For we are God's handiwork, created in Christ Jesus to do good works, which God prepared in advance for us to do."

MOVE #2: INVESTIGATE THE DESIGN

SHIFT #2: FROM MORE VOLUNTEERS ... TO MORE MASTERPIECES

BIG IDEA: THE CHURCH IS MADE TO BE MORE.

A core commitment of the local church is to help disciples investigate their masterpiece: their personal calling to a one-of-a-kind Masterpiece Mission for More. Every disciple is a unique, handcrafted-by-God vessel for expressing the fullness of Jesus into every corner of culture and into every sphere of society.

Pathway: This lesson consists of approximately one hour of advance preparation work for team members and a 75 to 90-minute interactive group gathering.

LESSON 02
MADE TO BE MORE ▶

PREPARATION BEFORE TEAM GATHERING

• Read Ephesians 2 and answer reflection questions. (10 minutes)

• Watch Video #4 – Rob Wegner and D.A. Horton on Ephesians 2 (25 minutes) and fill in the answers below.

• Watch Video #5 – Case Study of Westside Family Church (10 minutes) and write down at least one observation that captured your thinking.

• Read Lesson 2 and complete the discussion questions. (25 minutes)- Reflect on and answer the Introduction Discussion Questions.

   - Complete the questions in the church, team and personal assessment sections. These questions will be used for a rich conversation among team members during the team gathering. Be sure to invest time working through these assessment questions.

• Prayer – Spend some time praying that God will unify your team around a shared vision for seeing and mobilizing volunteers differently.

TEAM GATHERING

• Read Ephesians 2 together. (5 minutes)

• Discuss Introduction questions. (10 minutes)

• Watch Video #6 together – Léonce Crump. (25 minutes)

• Discuss Video #6 and Key Paradigm Thoughts. (10 minutes)

• Team Perspective and Assessment – Discuss assessment questions. (20 minutes)

• Shift #2 discussion and action. (15 minutes)

• Preview Lesson 3 expectations and prayer. (5 minutes)

INDIVIDUAL
PREPARATION ▶

LESSON 02
INDIVIDUAL PREP ▶

1. Read Ephesians 2. Like the previous lesson, pretend you've never experienced church and that what you read in Ephesians 2 is your first and only exposure to the characteristics of church. What conclusions or assumptions would you make about church?

2. Read Ephesians 2:10 again. Is this a promise for the church or for each individual believer?

3. What are the stewardship implications to each person being a masterpiece of God with a unique set of good deeds to accomplish?

4. What, in particular, about the passage convicted you personally about something in your life and leadership?

LESSON 02
MADE TO BE MORE ▶

Ephesians 2:8-10
"For it is by grace you have been saved, through faith - and this is not from yourselves, it is the gift of God - not by works, so that no one can boast. For we are God's handiwork, created in Christ Jesus to do good works, which God prepared in advance for us to do."

ROB WEGNER ON EPHESIANS 2

In Christ it is DONE, so we don't have to_____it.

Because it is done, we can now_____by GRACE the MORE we are CALLED TO!

We aren't just saved_____something.

We are saved_____something.

We are God's_____.

Ephesians 2:10
"For we are God's masterpiece. He has created us anew in Christ Jesus, so we can do the good things he planned for us long ago."

If we are going to see every nook and cranny of society filled with the fullness of Jesus, my responsibility as a leader is to help every disciple <u>discover</u> his or her one-of-a-kind Masterpiece Mission. It is the <u>multiplication</u> of these Masterpiece Missions that will create a beautiful mosaic to fill every corner of society with the fullness of Jesus.

MADE FOR MORE

MOVE #2: INVESTIGATE THE DESIGN

BIG IDEA: THE CHURCH IS MADE_____MORE.

This begins with every disciple of Jesus investigating his or her _____: how he or she is uniquely designed and called to one-of-a-kind Mission for More. All of us are vessels for carrying the fullness of Jesus to every nook and cranny of society.

MISHAPS IN MOBILIZATION: D.A. HORTON

P_____

Paternalism creates dependency and_____.

R_____

Simplifying mobilization to the_____needs of the body

Therefore, it devalues the_____of God.

I_____

Insecurity is when we are threatened by_____members.

D_____

The_____and_____distance between leadership, middle management and the laity.

E_____

When there is not community, people will feel like a_____.

CASE STUDY OF WESTSIDE FAMILY CHURCH *15 MINUTES*
WATCH VIDEO #5

In this video, you'll get to see how Westside Family Church is applying Move #2, Investigating the Design of More.

OBSERVATIONS:
Highlight at least one observation that really grabbed your attention from the video.

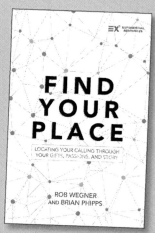

The G.P.S. personal calling discovery and deployment processed featured in this video will be available through the next book in the Exponential series, *Find Your Place: Locating Your Calling Through Gifts, Passions and Story* by Rob Wegner and Brian Phipps.

Release date: March 2019 at The Exponential Conference in Orlando, Florida.

In addition, a companion kit including:

... a weekend sermon series,

... small group materials,

... an online assessment for GPS with batch reporting of all church members within a congregation,

... an implementation guide for church leaders and

... a 30-minute coaching session with one of the authors will be available via the Find Your Place website and app at the time of the book's release. For more information now contact info@disciplesmade.com

LESSON 02
INDIVIDUAL PREP ▶

Review the Lesson 2 content from the past few pages (The Key Verses, the Move, the Shift, the Big Idea, your Notes from Ephesians and the Teaching Video Notes) and complete the following:

1. What stood out to you from the Lesson 2 reading material and videos? Why?

2. Flip forward to the Conversation Guide section, and review the questions in the church and team assessment inside the lesson. These questions will be used for deeper conversations among team members during the team gathering. Be sure to invest time reflecting on these assessment questions.

3. Personal Reflection: How well do I know my own Masterpiece Mission?

4. Personal Reflection: To what degree am I living out my Masterpiece Mission?

5. Personal Reflection: How well am I doing at revealing the fullness of Jesus where I live, work, study and play?

6. Spend some time praying that God will reveal needed changes in you, your team and your church. Pray that the upcoming gathering with your team will be transformational.

CONVERSATION
GUIDE

LESSON 02
CONVERSATION GUIDE ▶

Ephesians 2:8-10
"For it is by grace you have been saved, through faith - and this is not from yourselves, it is the gift of God - not by works, so that no one can boast. For we are God's handiwork, created in Christ Jesus to do good works, which God prepared in advance for us to do."

MOVE #2: INVESTIGATE THE DESIGN

SHIFT #2: FROM MORE VOLUNTEERS ... TO MORE MASTERPIECES

BIG IDEA: THE CHURCH IS MADE TO BE MORE.

A core commitment of the local church is to help disciples investigate their masterpiece: their personal calling to a one-of-a-kind Masterpiece Mission for More. Every disciple is a unique, handcrafted-by-God vessel for expressing the fullness of Jesus into every corner of culture and into every sphere of society.

The discussions in this study will be rich and fruitful. Stay mindful of the time as each question is only allotted 3 to 4 minutes. Fully engage the interaction with your team, but be careful not to dominate the conversation. Seek first to listen, allowing others to share their thoughts. Let your thinking be stimulated, but don't feel like the tension in every question needs to be relieved.

DISCUSSION QUESTIONS

1. Read Ephesians 2:10 together. Is this a promise for the church at large or for each follower of Jesus?

LESSON 02
MADE TO BE MORE ▶

2. Ephesians 2:10 is said to be the promise of a "sweet spot of personal calling." Every sweet spot in nature (and there are thousands) has a design, a purpose and a position. The intersection of these three dimensions is a sweet spot. People also have sweet spots of personal calling. We ask, "Who am I created to BE?" (a design question), "What am I made to DO?" (a purpose question), and "Where am I to GO to do it?" (a position question).

How does Ephesians 2:10 reflect these three dimensions of BE-DO-GO?

3. Every follower of Jesus is made to BE the unique masterpiece God designed them to be within the context of a healthy, biblical community of faith. If you were turning Ephesians 2:10 into a mission statement for mobilizing people in your church, how would you word it?

4. What stood out to you from the Lesson 2 reading, reflection questions and videos? Why?

LÉONCE CRUMP-MADE TO BE MORE   *30 MINUTES*
WATCH VIDEO #6 TOGETHER AS A TEAM.

IIIADE FOR MORE _____

LESSON 02
CONVERSATION GUIDE

After watching Video #6, read through the Key Paradigm Thoughts below as a team. Then, spend time talking through the Discussion Questions as a team.

Remember, a paradigm is what you think before you think about it. We'll never experience lasting change without examining those thoughts and allowing the Word and the Spirit to transform our assumptions.

Here are some key paradigm shifting ideas from Léonce Crump's talk Listen closely as we read these through.

KEY PARADIGM THOUGHT
THINK "FOR THEM," NOT, "FROM THEM."

When you think of what you want for people, how they serve your end becomes secondary to who they are becoming in Christ, the people they are meant to be.

KEY PARADIGM THOUGHT
DISTINGUISH DISCIPLESHIP FROM DEVELOPMENT.

Discipleship is helping them develop their character to become like Christ. Development is helping them discover their calling and living it out.

KEY PARADIGM THOUGHT
DISTINGUISH BIBLE KNOWLEDGE FROM A BIBLICAL WORLDVIEW.

Instead of just giving people Bible knowledge, equip them to let the Bible inform the way they see all things and function in the world.

LESSON 02
MADE TO BE MORE

KEY PARADIGM THOUGHT
SURFACE MINISTRY BOTTOM-UP, DON'T JUST PROGRAM MINISTRY TOP-DOWN.

"Encourage people to surface ministry for which you can equip them," versus "Developing ministries for which you must fill roles."

KEY PARADIGM THOUGHT
PREACH THE WHOLE GOSPEL.

"The Gospel is not a message of personal salvation but the total cosmic reorienting of all things!"

KEY PARADIGM THOUGHT
AUDACIOUS KINGDOM VISION

Have a vision so audacious that it pushes beyond the needs of "Running The Church," towards the dream of fulfilling "God's Kingdom Mission."

DISCUSSION QUESTIONS FROM LÉONCE CRUMP'S VIDEO

1. What challenged and confronted you the most?

2. What encouraged and comforted you the most?

3. What tensions are you feeling? Why?

MADE FOR MORE

LESSON 02
CONVERSATION GUIDE ▶

TEAM NOTES
Have someone on your team continue the "official set of notes" with your answers to the questions in this section and in the subsequent "Shift Section". Continue to build a comprehensive set of team notes for use in Lesson 7.

BIG IDEA: JESUS IS MORE! THE CHURCH IS MADE FOR MORE! THE CHURCH IS MADE TO BE MORE!

> *"Forward movement is not helpful if what is needed is a change of direction."- David Fleming*

> *"You can't depend on your eyes when your imagination is out of focus." - Mark Twain*

In this journey, we need the imagination to see beyond our current location and to be willing to question our current direction. Like the disciples on the walk to Emmaus, we can easily be blinded by preconceived notions that keep us from "seeing" how Jesus is at work right in front of us. It wasn't until Jesus "acted as if He was going on," that those disciples got desperate and begged him to break bread with them. At that moment, at the breaking of the bread, "their eyes were opened." (Luke 24)

In each part of the following team conversation, you are asked to look at your context but in a new way. Although two approaches will be presented as contrasts, *we fully acknowledge and celebrate the need for both*! However, we're asking you to consider: "Do you embrace both approaches? Is it balanced? Are you biased to one approach?" The dynamic tension we are creating is not an attack, but an opportunity to see something new.

LESSON 02
MADE TO BE MORE ▶

CHURCH ASSESSMENT

Remember, right now you are making a thoughtful, grace-filled and brutally honest assessment of your church, your team and your lives. You'll collect thoughts on how to apply this along the way, but you won't make any decision on your future direction until your final lesson.

1. Let's go back to our Home Depot motto from the Introduction. Take a minute and place a check mark next to each of the statements below that apply to your church.

THE "WE CAN BUILD IT. YOU CAN HELP." APPROACH TO INVESTIGATING THE DESIGN

☐ We help disciples Investigate their Design, so they can find a volunteer opportunity that intersects their God-given gifts, passions and story.

☐ First of all, the Ministry of the Church includes a wide-range of programs for people to participate in.

☐ The primary place for ministry is at our building or the locations of other organizations we partner with through programs and events. The direction of our church is "Come, join us!"

THE "YOU CAN BUILD IT. WE CAN HELP." APPROACH TO INVESTIGATING THE DESIGN OF MORE

☐ We will *equip* you, as a disciple of Jesus, to investigate your unique Design, so you can discover your one-of-a-kind Masterpiece Mission.

☐ First of all, the Ministry of the Church is all the people of God activated in their unique Masterpiece Missions, revealing the fullness of Jesus.

☐ The primary place for ministry is in every corner of culture and every sphere of society. The direction of our church is "Go and be!"

IIIADE FOR MOR≡

2. Which ones did you check? Unpack why.

3. How balanced are you between the two approaches? Which ones are you biased toward?

4. Approximately what percentage of your people have discovered their personal calling?

5. Approximately what percentage of your people are equipped and deployed into their unique personal calling?

6. What is your process to help people both live in common by serving the internal needs of the body and live deployed in their personal calling?

7. The Westside Family Church provided an example of how one movement is working out the approach of "You Can Build It. We Can Help." What were your impressions as you watched the Case Study of Westside?

LESSON 02
MADE TO BE MORE ▶

TEAM ASSESSMENT

1. How would you rate your commitment as a team to the "You Can Build It. We Can Help." approach of Investigating the Design?

2. What, if any, parts of P.R.I.D.E are holding you back?

PURSUING THE SHIFT: FROM MORE VOLUNTEERS ... TO MORE MASTERPIECES   *20 MINUTES*

TEAM NOTES
Add your team's conclusions in this section into the master list highlighted in the previous section.

The "Shift" section is intended to build on the previous Team Perspective section and help you start the process of moving from good ideas and intentions about "investigating the design" and shifting from "more volunteers" to "more masterpieces" into tangible action.

These six essential shifts collectively integrate to create a culture of Mobilization God's Way. In each of the six core lessons, you are looking at one shift to discern (1) where you are as a church today, (2) what mobilization in your church could look like in five years if you fully embraced the shift and (3) specific issues that would need to be addressed to make the shift successful.

In this lesson, you are focused on the shift:
FROM MORE VOLUNTEERS ... TO MORE MASTERPIECES!

The following exercise and questions are not intended to finalize your actions, but it is instead meant to get you thinking toward the future and unified on some core conclusions and convictions. You will be working through the six shifts leading up to your final lesson (Lesson 7) where you will seek to integrate what you've learned into a priority list of actions to investigate and pursue. For now, don't be limited by what you think you can and cannot do. Rather, dream about a future in which this shift becomes a reality.

 IIIADE FOR MOR≡

LESSON 02
CONVERSATION GUIDE ►

DISCUSSION QUESTIONS

1. Read through the following distinctions between **more volunteers** and **more masterpieces**. Assess where you are as a church on the spectrum of "more volunteers" versus "more masterpieces."

MORE VOLUNTEERS MEANS...

☐ Ministry equals volunteerism a few hours a month.

☐ Engaging ministry requires people to join a program of the local church or partner organization.

☐ Seeing the people as a means to an end to run the programs of the church and in so doing, fulfill "the vision" of "the church" that is defined corporately by a few.

MORE MASTERPIECES MEANS...

☐ Ministry equals all of life and happens mostly where we live, work, learn and play.

☐ Engaging ministry requires everyone to be a disciple who makes disciples first; and secondly, it requires disciples to fulfill their personal calling.

☐ Seeing the staff as the means to equip the people to discover their personal calling and deploying them to the best places for that calling.

2. Is this a shift that is worth the effort to pursue and to see put in place? How important is it to you? Why or why not?

3. In five years from now, if you were mobilizing God's people, God's way with an approach that was rooted in "more masterpieces" rather than "more volunteers," what would that look like? What would the characteristics of success be? What benefits? Create a list of characteristics that collectively describes a preferable future. 4. What challenges and obstacles would you face?

5. What specific issues do you know would need to be addressed?

6. Are there actions you already know you'd need to take that can be identified now? Any that you suspect are needed but need more investigation? Highlight them in your list.

AT THIS POINT, YOU'RE JUST COLLECTING IDEAS.
YOU SHOULDN'T MAKE ANY DECISIONS UNTIL LESSON 7.

NEXT WEEK

Next week we move on to Ephesians 3, Move #3 and Essential Shift #3. Be sure that you have the Participant's Guide for Lesson 3 and that you understand what work is to be completed before the next gathering.

• Read Ephesians 3 and Lesson 3. Journal your observations.

• Watch Video #7 (Rob Wegner and John Mark Comer on Ephesians 3).

• Watch Video #8 (Case Study of Bridgetown Church).

CLOSING PRAYER

IIIADE FOR MOR≡

MADE FOR MORE
LESSON 03

2019

VIDEOS CAN BE ACCESSED AT
EXPONENTIAL.ORG/MORE

LESSON 03
MADE TO LOVE MORE ▶

MADE TO LOVE MORE

SCRIPTURE - EPHESIANS 3

Ephesians 3:16-21
I pray that out of his glorious riches he may strengthen you with power through his Spirit in your inner being, so that Christ may dwell in your hearts through faith. And I pray that you, being rooted and established in love, may have power, together with all the Lord's holy people, to grasp how wide and long and high and deep is the love of Christ, and to know this love that surpasses knowledge - that you may be filled to the measure of all the fullness of God. Now to him who is able to do immeasurably more than all we ask or imagine, according to his power that is at work within us, to him be glory in the church and in Christ Jesus throughout all generations, for ever and ever! Amen.

MOVE #3: MOTIVATE WITH LOVE

SHIFT #3: FROM MORE GUILT ... TO MORE LOVE

BIG IDEA: THE CHURCH IS MADE TO LOVE MORE.

As we marinate in the love of God for us and in us, it will overflow through us. His love is the only sufficient motivation for our mission to More. To express the fullness of Jesus to others, we must have the fullness of Jesus in us. We grow in this fullness by being disciples ourselves (BE), who make disciples of others (DO), wherever we go (GO). This is the primary (general) calling all disciples have in common. Our personal (unique) calling, on the other hand, distinguishes us from all other disciples. The personal calling ONLY finds its significance within the context of our primary calling to be disciples, who make disciples, wherever we go.

Pathway: This lesson consists of approximately one hour of advance preparation work for team members and a 75 to 90-minute interactive group gathering.

 IIIADE FOR MORE

LESSON 03
MADE TO LOVE MORE ▶

- Read Ephesians 3 and answer reflection questions. (10 minutes)

- Watch Video #7 – Rob Wegner and John Mark Comer on Ephesians 3 (25 minutes) and fill in the answers below.

- Watch Video #8 – Case Study of Bridgetown Church (10 minutes) and write down at least one observation that captured your thinking.

- Read Lesson 3 and complete the discussion questions. (25 minutes)

    - Reflect on and answer the Introduction Discussion Questions.

    - Complete the questions in the church, team and personal assessment sections. These questions will be used for a rich conversation among team members during the team gathering. Be sure to invest time working through these assessment questions.

- Prayer – Spend some time praying for this week's team meeting.

TEAM GATHERING

- Read Ephesians 3 together. (5 minutes)

- Discuss Introduction questions. (10 minutes)

- Watch Video #9 together – Drew Hyun. (25 minutes)

- Discuss Video #9 and Key Paradigm Thoughts. (10 minutes)

- Team Perspective and Assessment – Discuss assessment questions. (20 minutes)

- Shift #3 discussion and action. (15 minutes)

- Preview Lesson 4 expectations and prayer. (5 minutes)

RESOURCE KIT
Lesson 3

INDIVIDUAL PREPARATION ▶

LESSON 03
INDIVIDUAL PREP

1. Read Ephesians 3. Like the previous lesson, pretend you've never experienced church and that what you read in Ephesians 3 is your first and only exposure to the characteristics of church. What conclusions or assumptions would you make about church?

2. Carrying the fullness of Jesus into every corner of society is our goal when mobilizing God's people, God's way. Ephesians 3:16-21 says that it is a foundation in love that positions us to be filled with the fullness of Jesus. What can happen when our motives for mobilization are rooted in anything other than love?

   Make a list of the different possible motives you have when recruiting volunteers. What causes you to have motives other than love?

3. What, in particular, about the passage convicted you personally about something in your life and leadership?

LESSON 03
MADE TO LOVE MORE

ROB WEGNER AND JOHN MARK COMER   *35 MINUTES*
ON EPHESIANS 3
COMPLETE THE FOLLOWING AS YOU WATCH VIDEO #7

EPHESIANS 3: ROB WEGNER

As a church leader, there is no way you can maintain the job of

exclusively motivating your people to be on_____.

BIG IDEA: The Church is Called_____More.

Paul is proclaiming that the fullness of Jesus' love_____

us, is and is alone the source for the fullness of Jesus to overflow

_____us.

Ephesians 3:14-19
For this reason I bow my knees before the Father, from whom every family in heaven and on earth is named, that according to the riches of his glory he may grant you to be strengthened with power through his Spirit in your inner being, so that Christ may dwell in your hearts through faith - that you, being rooted and grounded in love, may have strength to comprehend with all the saints what is the breadth and length and height and depth, and to know the love of Christ that surpasses knowledge, that you may be filled with all the fullness of God.

IIIADE FOR MOR三

ROOTED AND GROUNDED...

1. Being rooted is an_____Metaphor.

2. Being grounded is an_____Metaphor.

MOVE #3: MOTIVATE WITH LOVE

BIG IDEA: The Church is Called_____More.

SHIFT #3: FROM MORE GUILT ... TO MORE LOVE

EPHESIANS 3: JOHN MARK COMER

The Bridgetown Story

Trends at Bridgetown after Pursuing Missional for Five Years

1. The early adopters started to_____.

2. Some of our people got_____by the culture.

3. Most of our people were_____to join

   the movement.

BOTTOM LINE:
*"WE REALIZED WE DON'T JUST HAVE AN EVANGELISM
PROBLEM; WE HAVE A DISCIPLESHIP PROBLEM."*

LESSON 03
MADE TO LOVE MORE

If you separate mission from_____, then you have a surefire recipe for burn out.

The overarching word category for the church isn't <u>mission</u>; it's discipleship.

Discipleship is apprenticing to Jesus. That involves three dimensions:

1. The first is to be with Jesus. Jesus later called this lifestyle_____. If you don't have that baseline, you're dead in the water.

2. The second is to_____like Jesus. That's the end goal of apprenticeship.

3. The third is to do what Jesus would do if he were_____.

We can't put the cart before the horse. Mission is what you lead up to; it's not where you start.

Shift from emotionally_____to emotionally healthy.

Shift from discipleship as_____to discipleship as formation.

Teaching what Jesus commanded is different from teaching

_____obey what Jesus commanded them.

IIADE FOR MOR≡

LESSON 03
INDIVIDUAL PREP ▶

In this video, you'll get to see how Bridgetown Church is applying Move #3, Motivate with Love.

OBSERVATIONS:
Highlight at least one observation that really grabbed your attention from the video.

Review the Lesson 3 content from the past few pages *(The Key Verses, the Move, the Shift, the Big Idea, your Notes from Ephesians and the Teaching Video Notes)* and complete the following:

1. What stood out to you from the Lesson 3 reading material and videos? Why?

2. Flip forward to the Conversation Guide section, and review the questions in the **church and team assessment** inside the lesson. These questions will be used for deeper conversations among team members during the team gathering. Be sure to invest time reflecting on these assessment questions.

3. Personal Reflection: How well am I gospeling myself? How deeply am I receiving the love of God?

4. Personal Reflection: What are the shadow motivations of which I need to let the gospel heal me?

5. Personal Reflection:

How well am I doing at balancing general and secondary calling in my own life?

6. Spend some time praying that God will reveal needed changes in you, your team and your church and that the upcoming gathering with your team will be transformational.

CONVERSATION
GUIDE ▶

LESSON 03
MADE TO LOVE MORE ▶

Today we will jump into Ephesians 3.

Ephesians 3:16-21
I pray that out of his glorious riches he may strengthen you with power through his Spirit in your inner being, so that Christ may dwell in your hearts through faith. And I pray that you, being rooted and established in love, may have power, together with all the Lord's holy people, to grasp how wide and long and high and deep is the love of Christ, and to know this love that surpasses knowledge - that you may be filled to the measure of all the fullness of God. Now to him who is able to do immeasurably more than all we ask or imagine, according to his power that is at work within us, to him be glory in the church and in Christ Jesus throughout all generations, for ever and ever! Amen.

MOVE #3: MOTIVATE WITH LOVE

SHIFT #3: FROM MORE GUILT ... TO MORE LOVE

BIG IDEA: THE CHURCH IS MADE TO LOVE MORE.

As we marinate in the love of God for us and in us, it will overflow through us. His love is the only sufficient motivation for our mission to More. To express the fullness of Jesus to others, we must have the fullness of Jesus in us. We grow in this fullness by being disciples ourselves (BE), who make disciples of others (DO), wherever we go (GO). This is the primary (general) calling all disciples have in common. Our personal (unique) calling, on the other hand, distinguishes us from all other disciples. The personal calling ONLY finds its significance within the context of our primary calling to be disciples, who make disciples, wherever we go.

The discussions in this study will be rich and fruitful. Stay mindful of the time, as each question only has 3 to 4 minutes allotted. Fully engage the interaction with your team but be careful not to dominate the conversation. Seek first to listen, allowing others to share their thoughts. Let your thinking be stimulated, but don't feel like the tension in every question needs to be relieved.

ꟼADE FOR MORꟾ

LESSON 03
CONVERSATION GUIDE ▶

1. Read Ephesians 3 together. What are some of your observations about Jesus and the church?

2. Discuss the differences between primary or general calling and secondary or unique personal calling as described above. Why is it vitally important to distinguish the two callings? What happens when people focus on secondary or unique calling without understanding that our unique or secondary calling is given to support our primary calling?

3. How does love bind primary and secondary calling together? What could happen when other motives drive our pursuit of calling? What are some examples of improper motives by the church in mobilizing people?

4. What stood out to you from the Lesson 3 reading, reflection questions and videos? Why?

LESSON 03
MADE TO LOVE MORE ▶

DREW HYUN - MADE TO LOVE MORE	25 MINUTES
WATCH VIDEO #9 TOGETHER AS A TEAM.	

RETHINKING OUR PARADIGM	25 MINUTES
MOTIVATE WITH LOVE	

After watching Video #9, read through the Key Paradigm Thoughts below as a team. Then, spend time talking through the Discussion Questions as a team.

Remember, a paradigm is what you think before you think about it. You'll never experience lasting change without examining those thoughts and allowing the Word and the Spirit to transform your assumptions.

Here are some key paradigm shifting ideas from Drew Hyun's talk. Read through these as a team.

KEY PARADIGM THOUGHT

Every child of God has a general (primary) calling and a secondary (personal) calling. The primary calling is to be a disciple who can make disciples. The personal calling is to your one-of-a-kind Masterpiece Mission.

KEY PARADIGM THOUGHT

Secondary (personal) calling is under general (primary) calling. We need to mobilize followers of Jesus on their secondary calling. But, we should always keep the perspective that He gives us our secondary callings to fulfill our primary calling of making disciples who can make disciples. **Every disciple of Jesus has one message, the gospel, and one method, make disciples.** Every personal calling rests on the foundation of that primary calling. In fact, the moment we build our personal calling on anything else, it becomes an adventure in missing the point – a good thing that becomes a distraction from the main thing. **My personal calling must rest on the primary calling.**

KEY PARADIGM THOUGHT

Love is THE FOUNDATION for any calling to BE, DO, GO. What is the motivation for loving Jesus (the verb) and the loving Jesus (the adjective). The verb always follows the adjective. When you experience how loving (the adjective) Jesus is, you can't help but start loving (the verb) Jesus more. When you are certain of Jesus' love for you, Paul says that it is also like the foundation of a building or the roots of the tree (Ephesians 3:17).

For those who would like to take a closer look at the BE, DO, GO paradigm and the relationship between our primary and personal calling, be sure to check out the new book, *More: Find Your Personal Calling and Live Life to the Fullest Measure,* by Todd Wilson, founder and director of Exponential.

This book equips every Christian to discover his or her personal calling by answering three of the most important questions in life:

• Who am I created to be?

• What am I called to do?

• Where am I best positioned to do it?

This is a helpful resource to enable people to discover the who, what and where of calling as they engage in the journey God has for them. To learn more, visit more-book.com to download a free "Find Your Calling" Quick Start Guide and a complete sermon series guide to introduce the idea of personal calling to your church.

LESSON 03
MADE TO LOVE MORE ▶

1. What challenged and confronted you the most?

2. What encouraged and comforted you the most?

3. What tensions are you feeling? Why?

TEAM PERSPECTIVE   25 MINUTES
MOVE #3: MOTIVATE WITH LOVE

TEAM NOTES
Have someone on your team continue the "official set of notes" with your answers to the questions in this section and in the subsequent "Shift Section." Make it comprehensive and inclusive of the collective representation of your team. Seek to get as much unity of perspective as possible on your conclusions. Remember, these will be used to formulate a plan in Lesson 7.

LESSON 03
CONVERSATION GUIDE ▶

Gordon McKenzie, in his book, *Orbiting the Giant Hairball: A Corporate Fool's Guide to Surviving with Grace*, tells a childhood story recounting how he and his cousin learned to "mesmerize" chickens on his uncle's farm. First, they would grab a chicken and then hold its beak down to a white chalk line until it was "mesmerized." Believe it or not, the chickens would remain frozen staring at the line until the his uncle would come along and give them a kick in the backside.

With the Assessment Questions, we will ask you to look at your context, but not to be mesmerized by what you see there. Step back and try to see it in a new way. In other words, let Jesus give your current paradigm a kick in the backside! Two approaches will be presented as contrasts, but we fully acknowledge and celebrate the need for both! However, we're asking you to consider, "Do we embrace both approaches? Is it balanced? Is it lopsided? The dynamic tension we are creating is not an attack, but an opportunity to see something new.

CHURCH ASSESSMENT

Remember, right now you are making a thoughtful, grace-filled and brutally honest assessment of your church, your team and your lives. You'll collect thoughts on how to apply this along the way, but you won't make any decision on your future direction until your final lesson.

1. Let's go back to our Home Depot analogy from the Introduction. Take a minute and place a check mark next to each of the bulleted statements below that apply to your church (six total statements).

THE "WE CAN BUILD IT. YOU CAN HELP." APPROACH FOR MOTIVATE WITH LOVE

☐ We motivate by expressing needs with urgency and asking people to "make a difference".

☐ We have a strong emphasis on DO and GO.

☐ We equip disciples to flow in the Great Commission.

---

[1] Gordon McKenzie's book, *Orbiting the Giant Hairball: A Corporate Fool's Guide to Surviving with Grace*

LESSON 03
MADE TO LOVE MORE

THE "YOU CAN BUILD IT. WE CAN HELP." APPROACH FOR MOTIVATE WITH LOVE

- ☐ We motivate by first helping people understand how loved they are in Christ – that He has already "made the difference" they most need.

- ☐ We have a strong emphasis on BE, DO and GO.

- ☐ We equip disciples to flow in the Great Commission by understanding both their general (primary) calling to the Great Commission and their secondary (personal) calling to reveal the fullness of Jesus in every corner of culture and every sphere of society.

2. Which ones did you check? Unpack why.

3. How balanced are you between the two approaches? Which are you biased toward?

4. How do you motivate people to action and service? What are your primary motives? What messages are you intentionally and unintentionally sending to your people with these motives?

5. Approximately what percentage of your people are in a process to help them understand and experience the love of God in a way that is transformative – that deals with warped images of God, warped self-images, past wounds and unforgiveness?

IIIADE FOR MORE

6. Does your process help people discover and live in the proper balance of general (primary) calling and secondary (personal) calling?

TEAM ASSESSMENT

1. How would you rate your commitment as a team to the "You Can Build It. We Can Help." approach of Motivating with Love?

2. How would you rate your commitment as a team to helping every disciple discover both general (primary) and secondary (personal) calling?

PURSUING THE SHIFT: *15 MINUTES*
FROM MORE TO GUILT...TO MORE LOVE

TEAM NOTES
Add your team's conclusions in this section into the master list highlighted in the previous section.

The "Shift" section is intended to build on the previous Team Perspective section and help you start the process of moving from good ideas and intentions about "motivate with love" and shifting from "more guilt" to "more love" into tangible action.

LESSON 03
MADE TO LOVE MORE ▶

These six essential shifts collectively integrate to create a culture of Mobilization God's Way. In each of the six core lessons, we are looking at one shift to discern (1) where you are as a church today, (2) what mobilization in your church could look like in five years if you fully embraced the shift and (3) specific issues that would need to be addressed to make the shift successful.

In this lesson, you are focused on the shift:
FROM MORE GUILT ... TO MORE LOVE!

The following exercise and questions are not intended to finalize your actions, but it is instead meant to get you thinking toward the future and unified on some core conclusions and convictions. You will be working through the six shifts leading up to your final lesson (Lesson 7) where you will seek to integrate what you've learned into a priority list of actions to investigate and pursue. For now, don't be limited by what you think you can and cannot do. Instead dream about a future in which this shift becomes a reality.

DISCUSSION QUESTIONS

1. Read through the following distinctions between **more guilt** and **more love**. Assess where you are as a church on the spectrum of "more guilt" versus "more love."

MORE GUILT MEANS...

☐ The staff continually needs to "pump" people up to fill the necessary slots.

☐ The people feel that ministry is something they "should" do. Once a year, we do a big campaign to recruit people.

☐ Seasonal burnout of volunteers is the norm. The burnout is not addressed proactively through spiritual formation as the priority. Rather, it is addressed reactively by telling people to take a break; and then, a new volunteer is sought out to take their place.

IIIADE FOR MOR≡

LESSON 03
CONVERSATION GUIDE

MORE LOVE MEANS...

☐ Our first concern as leaders is that we are abiding in the presence of Jesus and resting in His love. Our first concern for those we lead is to equip them to know HOW TO abide in Jesus.

☐ The people feel that ministry is the natural overflow of their life with Jesus, and it's the highest honor to join Jesus on His mission where they live, work, learn and play. People are constantly taking new steps in ministry without the need for big external pressure.

☐ We practice daily, weekly and annual rhythms of work and rest that keep us in sync with God's design for us, embodied in the life of Jesus.

2. Is this a shift that is worth the effort to pursue and to see put in place? How important is it to you? Why or why not?

3. In five years from now, if you were mobilizing God's people, God's way with an approach that was rooted in "more love" rather than "more effort," what would that look like? What would the characteristics be of success? What benefits? Create a list of characteristics that collectively describes a preferable future.

LESSON 03
MADE TO LOVE MORE ▶

4. What challenges and obstacles would you face?

What specific issues do you know would need to be addressed?

Are there actions you already know you'd need to take that can be identified now? Are there any that you suspect are needed but require more investigation? Highlight them in your list.

AT THIS POINT, YOU'RE JUST COLLECTING IDEAS.
YOU SHOULDN'T MAKE ANY DECISIONS UNTIL LESSON 7.

NEXT WEEK

Next week, we move on to Ephesians 4, Move #4 and Essential Shift #4. Be sure that you have the Participant's Guide for Lesson 4 and that you understand what work is to be completed before the next gathering.

• **Read Ephesians 4 and Lesson 4.** Journal your observations.

• **Watch Video #10** (Rob Wegner and Brian Sanders on Ephesians 4).

• **Watch Video #11** (Case Study of Tampa Underground Church).

CLOSING PRAYER

 IIIADE FOR MOR⹂

MADE FOR MORE
LESSON 04

2019

LESSON 04
MADE TO DO MORE

▶

MADE TO DO MORE

SCRIPTURE - EPHESIANS 4

Ephesians 4:11-16
So Christ himself gave the apostles, the prophets, the evangelists, the pastors and teachers, to equip his people for works of service, so that the body of Christ may be built up until we all reach unity in the faith and in the knowledge of the Son of God and become mature, attaining to the whole measure of the fullness of Christ. Then we will no longer be infants, tossed back and forth by the waves, and blown here and there by every wind of teaching and by the cunning and craftiness of people in their deceitful scheming. Instead, speaking the truth in love, we will grow to become in every respect the mature body of him who is the head, that is, Christ. From him the whole body, joined and held together by every supporting ligament, grows and builds itself up in love, as each part does its work.

MOVE #4: ORGANIZE FOR FULLNESS

SHIFT #4: FROM MORE HIERARCHY TO MORE MISSIONARIES

BIG IDEA: THE CHURCH IS MADE TO DO MORE.

Just as the body has systems that work together to allow for health and reproduction, Jesus gives organizing systems to His body for fullness, for more impact, and for the mobilization of EVERY member. Jesus has provided a mosaic of unique gifts as represented within the five-fold gifting of APEST. Regardless of our theology on these gifts, we are wise to at least consider the pragmatic wisdom in the strengths represented within these gifts. Without representation these strengths, we will struggle to express His fullness into every corner of culture and into every sphere of society. We must see the unique roles and gifts given by Jesus as an important organizing system in the body of Christ.

Pathway: This lesson consists of approximately one hour of advance preparation work for team members and a 75 to 90-minute interactive group gathering.

IIIADE FOR MORE

LESSON 04
MADE TO DO MORE ▶

PREPARATION BEFORE TEAM GATHERING

• Read Ephesians 4 and answer reflection questions. (10 minutes)

• Watch Video #10 – Rob Wegner and Brian Sanders on Ephesians 4 (25 minutes) and fill in the answers below.

• Watch Video #11 – Case Study of Tampa Underground Church (10 minutes) and write down at least one observation that captured your thinking.

• Read Lesson 4 and complete the discussion questions. (25 minutes)

  - Reflect on and answer the Introduction Discussion Questions.

  - Complete the questions in the church, team and personal assessment sections. These questions will be used for a rich conversation among team members during the team gathering. Be sure to invest time working through these assessment questions.

• Prayer - Spend some time praying for this week's team training.

TEAM GATHERING

• Read Ephesians 4 together. (5 minutes)

• Discuss Introduction questions. (10 minutes)

• Watch Video #12 together – Alan Hirsch. (25 minutes)

• Discuss Video #12 and Key Paradigm Thoughts. (10 minutes)

• Team Perspective and Assessment – Discuss assessment questions. (20 minutes)

• Shift #4 discussion and action. (15 minutes)

• Preview Lesson 5 expectations and prayer. (5 minutes)

RESOURCE KIT

Lesson 4

INDIVIDUAL
PREPARATION

LESSON 04
INDIVIDUAL PREP ▶

1. Read Ephesians 4. Like the previous lesson, pretend you've never experienced church and that what you read in Ephesians 4 is your first and only exposure to the characteristics of church. What conclusions or assumptions would you make about church?

   How would you put Ephesians 4:11-16 into practice? Would you organize around it? Why or why not?

2. What, in particular, about the passage convicted you personally about something in your life and leadership?

   We acknowledge that there has been and continues to be differences of opinion within the church over the "5-Fold Gifts" mentioned in Ephesians 4. Were they only for the early church? Are the Apostolic and Prophetic gifts only for the first century? Were these 5 gifts only reserved for a few people who then equip others OR is the entire church blessed with a spectrum of these functional gifts? These questions of cessationism or continualism have been debated for years. Are we likely to resolve with perfect unity the application of the 5-fold gifts to the church today? No and we don't need to. Instead of focusing on what we can't get unity on, let's focus on where we can be united.

LESSON 04
MADE TO DO MORE ▶

For this study, we will live in the dynamic tension of the different interpretations of Ephesians 4, while placing our focus on the very pragmatic, underlying strengths and functions of each gift:

- Pioneering, sending, extending, and entrepreneurial (Apostolic).
- Questioning systems of power, seeking justice, critiquing mission drift, and protecting the marginalized (Prophetic).
- Reaching out, including the seeker, proclaiming the Gospel, and Including new people (Evangelistic).
- Nurture, care, community and health (Shepherding).
- Sound doctrine, clear teaching, effective processes and systems, and strong values (Teaching).

Functionally, let us suggest these are roles EVERY healthy organization needs. If we were starting a company, would these aforementioned underlying strengths be a good way to organize? Yes. Did Jesus through Paul call out these strengths and acknowledge there relevance? Yes. Did Jesus directly command ("Thou shalt...") that we organize directly around them in a specific prescriptive way? No. Were those strengths vital to the early church? Yes. Is there wisdom in us at least pragmatically considering how the strengths play into how we organize for mobilization? Absolutely. If we can agree to all those things, can we then also agree that it makes sense that we need some form of intentional design in our churches for MOST EFFECTIVELY MOBILIZING GOD'S PEOPLE GOD'S WAY? In that light, let's consider the wisdom of Ephesians 4 together.

ROB WEGNER AND BRIAN SANDERS ON EPHESIANS 4   *25 MINUTES*
COMPLETE THE FOLLOWING AS YOU WATCH VIDEO #10

EPHESIANS 4: ROB WEGNER

Ephesians 4:11-13
So, Christ himself gave the apostles, the prophets, the evangelists, the pastors and teachers, to equip his people for works of service, so that the body of Christ may be built up until we all reach unity in the faith and in the knowledge of the Son of God and become mature, attaining to the whole measure of the fullness of Christ.

IⅡADE FOR MOR三 _____

LESSON 04
INDIVIDUAL PREP

BIG IDEA:

The Church is Made to_____. Jesus has provided the

organization to release the More in His body: The Five-Fold Gifting of

_____.

MOVE #4:
ORGANIZE FOR_____.

WHY?

It is so that the church might be built up, so it might reach unity, become

mature and reach the measure of the_____of Christ.

Fullness is the goal!

THE THREE LAYERS OF FULLNESS IN EPHESIANS

LAYER ONE - _____ FULLNESS: Ephesians 1

LAYER TWO - _____ FULLNESS: Ephesians 3

LAYER THREE - _____ FULLNESS: Ephesians 2 & 4

LESSON 04
MADE TO DO MORE

HOW?

Jesus has given us vitally important gifts; and when they are activated

and respected, these_____influencing styles will empower

the Church to reach its FULL_____.

The **APOSTLE** is one who_____and expands.

The **PROPHET** is one who_____and critiques.

The **EVANGELIST** is the one who recruits to the cause.

The **SHEPHERD** who_____and provide the
nurturer.

The **TEACHER** is one who_____and organizes.

Let's see the fivefold giftings as organizing_____in
the Church.

Think of the collective strengths and characteristics represented within
each of the five-fold gifts of APEST as a 'system' How many of the five
systems function in a synergistic way in your local church?

LESSON 04
INDIVIDUAL PREP

APEST AS A CATALYST FOR MOVEMENT: BRIAN SANDERS

Don't just think of APEST in terms of your leadership team. That's too

_____.

The real leadership team of your church are the people leading on the front lines of mission. The ones stepping into the fight on a daily basis.

It's more important to see APEST at work on the front lines than in the administrative team who supports them.

These five gifts represent the fronts on which we fight.

The **APOSTLE:**_____Ground

The **PROPHET:** Injustice

The **EVANGELIST:**_____

The **SHEPHERD:** Brokenness

The **TEACHER:**_____

The church is a_____organism. It cannot be

controlled, and it cannot be killed. It isn't a_____to

be managed but a_____to be released.

LESSON 04
MADE TO DO MORE ▸

In this next video, you'll see a case study of a church, Tampa Underground, that is organizing around APEST in a creative and organic way. They see it as a natural expression of being the body of Christ. One thing we all agree on: We are called to become like Jesus and the church is His Body. Without a doubt, Jesus functioned in all five giftings. Was Jesus an apostle? Yes! Was he a prophet? Yes! An evangelist? Better than Billy, God rest his soul. A shepherd? Yes. A teacher? The best ever. If we are His body, we must at least consider how the underlying strengths of these gifts are manifested in us and through the Body of the local church. Let us consider the example of Tampa Underground as they seek to follow Jesus and become like him in this way.

In this video, you'll get to see how Tampa Underground Church is applying Move #4, Organize for Fullness.

OBSERVATIONS:
Highlight at least one observation that really grabbed your attention from the video.

READ LESSON 4, REFLECT AND PRAY   25 MINUTES

Review the Lesson 4 content from the past few pages (The Key Verses, the Move, the Shift, the Big Idea, your notes from Ephesians and the Teaching Video Notes) and complete the following:

1. What stood out to you from the Lesson 4 reading material and videos? Why?

LESSON 04
INDIVIDUAL PREP

2. Flip forward to the Conversation Guide section, and review the questions in the church and team assessment inside the lesson. These questions will be used for deeper conversations among team members during the team gathering. Be sure to invest time reflecting on these assessment questions.

3. How well do you know your own Influencing Style from APEST?

4. How well do you work together with others around APEST?

5. To what degree are you helping others discover their influencing style?

6. Spend some time praying about what God has been revealing to you in this study. Pray for your teammates and for your upcoming gathering.

CONVERSATION
GUIDE ▸

LESSON 04
CONVERSATION GUIDE ▶

Today we will jump into Ephesians 4.

Ephesians 4:11-16
So, Christ himself gave the apostles, the prophets, the evangelists, the pastors and teachers, to equip his people for works of service, so that the body of Christ may be built up until we all reach unity in the faith and in the knowledge of the Son of God and become mature, attaining to the whole measure of the fullness of Christ. Then we will no longer be infants, tossed back and forth by the waves, and blown here and there by every wind of teaching and by the cunning and craftiness of people in their deceitful scheming. Instead, speaking the truth in love, we will grow to become in every respect the mature body of him who is the head, that is, Christ. From him the whole body, joined and held together by every supporting ligament, grows and builds itself up in love, as each part does its work.

MOVE #4: ORGANIZE FOR FULLNESS

SHIFT #4: FROM MORE HIERARCHY ... TO MORE MISSIONARIES

BIG IDEA: THE CHURCH IS MADE TO DO MORE.

Just as the body has systems that work together to allow for health and reproduction, Jesus gives organizing systems to His body for fullness, for more impact and for the mobilization of EVERY member. Jesus has provided a mosaic of unique gifts as represented within the five-fold gifting of APEST. Regardless of our theology on these gifts, we are wise to at least consider the pragmatic wisdom in the strengths represented within these gifts. Without representation these strengths, we will struggle to express His fullness into every corner of culture and into every sphere of society. We must see the unique roles and gifts given by Jesus as an important organizing system in the body of Christ.

The discussions in this study will be rich and fruitful. Stay mindful of the time as each question only has 3 to 4 minutes allotted. Fully engage the interaction with your team, but be careful not to dominate the conversation. Seek first to listen, allowing others to share their thoughts. Let your thinking be stimulated, but don't feel like the tension in every question needs to be relieved.

Conversation Guide | **RESOURCE KIT**

Lesson 4

LESSON 04
MADE TO DO MORE

1. Read Ephesians 4 together. What are some of your observations about Jesus and the church?

2. There are leaders who believe the five-fold gifts in Ephesians 4 were only for the early church. There are others who believe it's a significant missing piece in church today. Where do you stand as a team on this spectrum of views?

3. When you look inside a large growing company (ministry or secular), you see many critical roles such as visionary leadership, R&D, engineering, quality control, training, marketing, branding, etc. In what ways are the underlying characteristics in APEST an expression of the natural roles needed for growing any organization?

LESSON 04
CONVERSATION GUIDE ►

4. For this question, assume Jesus did intend for churches to have the full mosaic of the functional strengths representing by the different giftings mentions in Ephesians 4. How is your team doing? Do your teams naturally migrate to having these gifts even when you are not intentional? Here's quick review of those functional strengths:

- Pioneering, sending, extending, and entrepreneurial (Apostolic).

- Questioning systems of power, seeking justice, critiquing mission drift, and protecting the marginalized (Prophetic).

- Reaching out, including the seeker, proclaiming the Gospel, and Including new people (Evangelistic).

- Nurture, care, community and health (Shepherding).

- Sound doctrine, clear teaching, effective processes and systems, and strong values (Teaching).

5. Church leaders often cite Ephesians 4:11-16 as the justification for paid staff to be equippers of others who do ministry. As these verses progress, we are given the real reason why Jesus gives the gifts. The equipping of others for works of service is actually a means to the ultimate end. What is the ultimate end?

6. Do you see the connection between this ultimate end (fullness and maturity in the body) and our key verses in Ephesians 1:22-23?

7. What is the consequence when followers of Jesus do not discover and engage their unique sweet spot of personal calling, which is given by Jesus so that each person can play his or her unique role in the mission for the church?

8. Our responsibility as leaders is to intentionally organize roles and teams to see the fullness of Jesus carried into every corner of society as the fruit! When we fail to do this, we limit our members from discovering and engaging their unique roles.

9. What stood out to you from the Lesson 4 reading, reflection questions and videos? Why?

ALAN HIRSCH - EPHESIANS 4   *25 MINUTES*
WATCH VIDEO #12 TOGETHER AS A TEAM.

Without a doubt, Alan Hirsch has been one of the leading voices on this topic, calling the church to reimagine herself as a movement, not an institution, energized by the leadership gifts and functions in APEST. Frank Herbert once said, "The best prophets lead you up to the curtain and let you peer through for yourself." Alan is inviting us to peer behind the curtain of Ephesians 4 with new eyes. We are including his voice, not to create a new theology or debate, but instead to challenge us to ponder the pragmatic wisdom of APEST in informing the organizing systems in the church. We acknowledge and affirm differing theological positions on this passage and are not taking a specific theological position.

IIIADE FOR MOR☰

LESSON 04
CONVERSATION GUIDE ▶

After watching Video #12, read through the Key Paradigm Thoughts below as a team. Then, spend time talking through the Discussion Questions as a team.

Remember, a paradigm is what you think before you think about it. You'll never experience lasting change without examining those thoughts and allowing the Word and the Spirit to transform your assumptions.

Here are some key paradigm shifting ideas from Alan Hirsch's talk. Listen closely as you read through these thoughts.

KEY PARADIGM THOUGHT

MOX *(Ministry of Christ)* > **BOX** *(Body of Christ)* > **FOX** *(Fullness of Christ)*

MINISTRY OF CHRIST:
Was Jesus an Apostle? A Prophet? An Evangelist? A Shepherd? A Teacher? Yes!

BODY OF CHRIST:
If Jesus is the Head of His Body, the Church, will APEST continue to be expressed through His Body? Yes!

FULLNESS OF CHRIST:
If we are missing one of these organizing systems as a local church, then we are lacking the fullness of Christ.

KEY PARADIGM THOUGHT
APEST ARE ALSO MARKS OF THE CHURCH.

As we have seen, based on the dynamic presence of Christ, every church needs to have all five gifts active to fully function as the Body of Christ. In other words, these are very viable marks of the church. Another way of saying marks is metrics. APEST is a realistic dashboard of organizing for fullness.

KEY PARADIGM THOUGHT
THE TWO TRIANGLES

Take a minute to examine the two triangles...

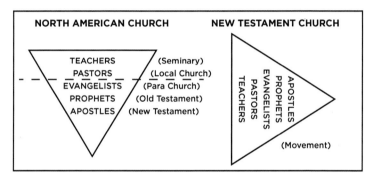

| NORTH AMERICAN CHURCH | NEW TESTAMENT CHURCH |

TEACHERS (Seminary)
PASTORS (Local Church)
EVANGELISTS (Para Church)
PROPHETS (Old Testament)
APOSTLES (New Testament)

APOSTLES PROPHETS EVANGELISTS PASTORS TEACHERS

(Movement)

DISCUSSION QUESTIONS FROM ALAN HIRSCH'S VIDEO

1. What challenged and confronted you the most?

2. What encouraged and comforted you the most?

3. What tensions are you feeling? Why?

IIIADE FOR MOR≡

LESSON 04
CONVERSATION GUIDE ▶

TEAM NOTES
Have someone on your team continue the "official set of notes" with your answers to the questions in this section and in the subsequent "Shift Section." By this time, you should see the value in having these comprehansice notes.

BIG IDEA: JESUS IS MORE! THE CHURCH IS MADE FOR MORE! THE CHURCH IS MADE TO BE MORE! THE CHURCH IS MADE TO DO MORE!

*"The voyage of discovery is not in seeking
new landscapes but in having new eyes."*
- Marcel Proust

*"All truth passes through three stages.
First, it is ridiculed. Second, it is violently opposed.
Third, it is accepted as being self-evident"*
- Arthur Schopenhauer

Leadership guru Max De Pree famously said, "The first job of a leader is to define reality." Jesus gets the privilege of decisively defining the Church, including these organizing systems found in Ephesians 4. As church leaders, we need to take this task of shaping the way people think about the church with utmost seriousness. Allowing Jesus to guide us, it is part of the leadership task to help our local churches see the Church as Jesus does.

In each part of the following team conversation, you are asked to look at your context but in a new way. Although two approaches will be presented as contrasts, we fully acknowledge and celebrate the need for both! However, we're asking you to consider: "Do you embrace both approaches? Is it balanced? Are you biased to one approach?" The dynamic tension we are creating is not an attack, but an opportunity to see something new.

LESSON 04
MADE TO DO MORE ▶

CHURCH ASSESSMENT

1. Let's go back to our Home Depot analogy from the Introduction. Take a minute and place a check mark next to each of the bulleted statements below that apply to your church (six total bullets).

THE "WE CAN BUILD IT. YOU CAN HELP."
APPROACH FOR ORGANIZING FOR FULLNESS

☐ We organize around the one or two of the functions describe in Ephesians 4 listed here. Typically, these one or two rise to the top because they are the couple that our pastor, leadership team or denomination are most passionate and comfortable with.

- Pioneering, sending, extending, and entrepreneurial (Apostolic).
- Questioning systems of power, seeking justice, critiquing mission drift, and protecting the marginalized (Prophetic).
- Reaching out, including the seeker, proclaiming the Gospel, and Including new people (Evangelistic).
- Nurture, care, community and health (Shepherding).
- Sound doctrine, clear teaching, effective processes and systems, and strong values (Teaching).

☐ Our primary dashboard is built around the ABC's (Attendance, Baptisms, and Cash) of the Church.

☐ We only equip disciples for the one or two functions about which our pastor, team or denomination are most passionate or comfortable.

THE "YOU CAN BUILD IT. WE CAN HELP."
APPROACH FOR ORGANIZING FOR FULLNESS

☐ We organize around all five roles of APEST for the purpose of releasing the fullness of Jesus.

☐ Our primary dashboard is built around metrics for each of the organizing systems (APEST) in Ephesians 4.

☐ We equip every disciple to discovery their primary influencing style from Ephesians 4 and encourage them to appreciate all the others as necessary.

IIIADE FOR MOR≡

LESSON 04
CONVERSATION GUIDE

2. Which ones did you check? Unpack why.

3. Which of the these five functions do you think is your church's greatest strength? Which is your church's greatest weakness?

- Pioneering, sending, extending, and entrepreneurial *(Apostolic)*.

- Questioning systems of power, seeking justice, critiquing mission drift, and protecting the marginalized *(Prophetic)*.

- Reaching out, including the seeker, proclaiming the Gospel, and Including new people *(Evangelistic)*.

- Nurture, care, community and health *(Shepherding)*.

- Sound doctrine, clear teaching, effective processes and systems, and strong values *(Teaching)*.

4. How well are you organized around all five organizing roles? Which is the one that receives the most emphasis? Which ones are mostly ignored?

5. What is your current scoreboard? How could it better express all five organizing systems?

LESSON 04
MADE TO DO MORE ▶

TEAM ASSESSMENT

1. How would you rate your commitment as a team to the "You Can Build It. We Can Help" approach of Organizing for Fullness?

2. What, if any, are the obstacles that would keep you from Organizing for Fullness?

PURSUING THE SHIFT: FROM MORE HIERARCHY .... TO MORE MISSIONARIES   *15 MINUTES*

TEAM NOTES
Add your team's conclusions in this section into the master list highlighted in the previous section.

In this lesson, we are focused on the shift:
From More Hierarchy ... to More Missionaries!

The following exercise and questions are not intended to finalize your actions, but it is instead meant to get you thinking toward the future and unified on some core conclusions and convictions. You will be working through the six shifts leading up to your final lesson (Lesson 7) where you will seek to integrate what you've learned into a priority list of actions to investigate and pursue. For now, don't be limited by what you think you can and cannot do. Rather, dream about a future in which this shift becomes a reality.

 IIIADE FOR MOR☰

LESSON 04
CONVERSATION GUIDE ▶

1. Read through the following distinctions between **more hierarchy** and **more missionaries**. Assess where you are as a church on the spectrum of "more hierarchy" versus "more missionaries."

MORE HIERARCHY MEANS...

☐ The pastors and staff lead and define all the ministry, and the members support that work.

☐ New "ministries" of the church always have to "go up the chain" before anything can be done.

☐ The staff is evaluated by how effective their ministry is.

MORE MISSIONARIES MEANS...

☐ All members see their lives, where they live, work, learn and play, as their main ministry. In addition, they are excited to the contribute to the shared ministry of the church through centralized programs.

☐ Members are launching new ministry initiatives all the timewithout expectation that "the church" will do it for them, pay for it or centralize it.

☐ The staff is evaluated by how effectively they are equipping others in their ministry to the body and their mission in the world.

2. Is this a shift that is worth effort pursuing that you'd want to see put in place? How important is it to you? Why or why not?

3. In five years from now, if you were mobilizing God's people God's way with an approach that was rooted in "more missionaries" rather than "more hierarchy," what would that look like? What would the characteristics of success be? What benefits? Create a list of characteristics that collectively describes a preferable future.

4. What challenges and obstacles would you face?

5. What specific issues do you know would need to be addressed?

LESSON 04
CONVERSATION GUIDE ▶

6. Are there actions you already know you'd need to take that can be identified now?

7. Are there any that you suspect are needed but require more investigation? Highlight them in your list.

AT THIS POINT, YOU'RE JUST COLLECTING IDEAS.
YOU SHOULDN'T MAKE ANY DECISIONS UNTIL LESSON 7.

NEXT WEEK

Next week, we move on to Ephesians 5, Move #5 and Essential Shift #5. Be sure that you have the Participant's Guide for Lesson 5 and that you understand what work is to be completed before the next gathering.

• **Read Ephesians 5 and Lesson 5.** Journal your observations.

• **Watch Video #13** (Rob Wegner and Danielle Strickland on Ephesians 4).

• **Watch Video #14** (Highlights of Mobilization from four case study churches).

CLOSING PRAYER

MADE FOR MORE

LESSON 05

2019

VIDEOS CAN BE ACCESSED AT
EXPONENTIAL.ORG/MORE

MADE TO GO MORE

SCRIPTURE - EPHESIANS 5

Ephesians 5:8, 14-17
For you were once darkness, but now you are light in the Lord. Live as children of light... This is why it is said: "Wake up, sleeper, rise from the dead, and Christ will shine on you." Be very careful, then, how you live - not as unwise but as wise, making the most of every opportunity, because the days are evil. Therefore, do not be foolish, but understand what the Lord's will is.

MOVE #5: ACTIVATE ALL THE PEOPLE ON PURPOSE

SHIFT #5: FROM MORE PROGRAMS ... TO MORE MISSION FIELDS

BIG IDEA: THE CHURCH IS MADE TO GO MORE.

The people of God have already been sent and placed strategically by Jesus. Mission begins by expressing the fullness of Jesus where we live, work, study, and play. Every disciple is a missionary with a unique mission field, their mosaic of mission. All those overlapping mosaics of mission are Jesus' plan to express His fullness into every corner of culture and into every sphere of society. Each mosaic significantly extends the "footprint of fullness." Our "GO" is to embrace our mission field and "make the most of every opportunity" to express the FULLNESS of Jesus to others.

Pathway: This lesson consists of approximately one hour of advance preparation work for team members and a 75 to 90-minute interactive group gathering.

MADE FOR MORE

LESSON 05
MADE TO GO MORE ▶

• Read Ephesians 5 and answer reflection questions. (10 minutes)

• Watch Video #13 – Rob Wegner and Danielle Strickland on Ephesians 5 (30 minutes) and fill in the answers below.

• Watch Video #14 – Case Studies of Several Featured Churches (10 minutes) and write down at least one observation that captured your thinking.

• Read Lesson 5 and complete the discussion questions. (25 minutes)

  - Reflect on and answer the Introduction Discussion Questions.

  - Complete the questions in the church, team and personal assessment sections. These questions will be used for a rich conversation among team members during the team gathering. Be sure to invest time working through these assessment questions.

• Prayer – Spend some time praying for this week's team meeting.

TEAM GATHERING

• Read Ephesians 5 together. (5 minutes)

• Discuss Introduction questions. (10 minutes)

• Watch Video #15 together – Tampa Underground Documentary. (25 minutes)

• Discuss Video #15 and Key Paradigm Thoughts. (10 minutes)

• Team Perspective and Assessment – discuss assessment questions. (20 minutes)

• Shift #5 discussion and action. (15 minutes)

• Preview Lesson 6 expectations and prayer. (5 minutes)

INDIVIDUAL PREPARATION

LESSON 05
INDIVIDUAL PREP ▶

1. Read Ephesians 5. Like the previous lesson, pretend you've never experienced church and that what you read in Ephesians 5 is your first and only exposure to the characteristics of church. What conclusions or assumptions would you make about church?

2. What does "making the most of every opportunity" mean to you? Do you see yourself as a missionary with a unique mission field to carry the fullness of Jesus into your unique corners of society? Do the people in your area of influence see themselves as missionaries to a unique mission field who are commanded to make the most of every opportunity?

3. What, in particular, about the passage convicted you personally about something in your life and leadership?

ROB WEGNER & DANIELLE STRICKLAND   *30 MINUTES*
ON EPHESIANS 5
COMPLETE THE FOLLOWING AS YOU WATCH VIDEO #13.

LESSON 05
MADE TO GO MORE

EPHESIANS 5: ROB WEGNER

Ephesians 5:8,14-17
For you were once darkness, but now you are light in the Lord. Live as children of light... This is why it is said: "Wake up, sleeper, rise from the dead, and Christ will shine on you." Be very careful, then, how you live - not as unwise but as wise, making the most of every opportunity, because the days are evil. Therefore, do not be foolish, but understand what the Lord's will is.

BIG IDEA:

The Church is Made to_____More. The people of God

have already been sent and placed strategically by Jesus.

MOVE #5: ACTIVATE ALL THE_____
ON PURPOSE.

SHIFT #5: FROM MORE PROGRAMS ...
TO MORE MISSION FIELDS

AWAKENING AGENTS: DANIELLE STRICKLAND

The spiders represent a spiritual sleepiness.

In the garden, Jesus is about to do something EPIC; the disciples

are_____.

If we give into the sleepy spirit, we get consumed by tiny, insignificant things that don't even matter.

_____is the agent that wakes up everyone.

The agent that has woken me most from my slumber

is_____.

IIIADE FOR MOR≡ _____

LESSON 05
INDIVIDUAL PREP ▶

In this video, you'll get to see how several churches are sending people on mission and applying Move #5, Activate All the People on Purpose.

OBSERVATIONS:
Highlight at least one observation that really grabbed your attention from the video.

READ LESSON 5, REFLECT AND PRAY   *25 MINUTES*

Review the Lesson 5 content from the past few pages (The Key Verses, the Move, the Shift, the Big Idea, your Notes from Ephesians and the Teaching Video Notes) and complete the following:

1. What stood out to you from the Lesson 5 reading material and videos? Why?

2. Flip forward to the Conversation Guide section, and review the questions in the church and team assessment inside the lesson. These questions will be used for deeper conversations among team members during the team gathering. Be sure to invest time reflecting on these assessment questions...

3. How awake are you to the mission of God where you live, work, study and play? Do you see yourself as a missionary to a unique mission field in your unique corners of society?

4. What does (or could) it look like for you to "make the most of every opportunity" as a missionary to your unique mission fields where you work, live and play?

5. To what degree are you helping others discover their influencing style?

6. Spend some time praying about what God has been revealing to you in this study. Pray for your teammates and for your upcoming gathering.

7. Spend some time praying that God will reveal new mission field opportunities for you.

CONVERSATION GUIDE

LESSON 05
MADE TO GO MORE ▶

Today we will jump into Ephesians 5.

> **Ephesians 5:8,14-17**
> *For you were once darkness, but now you are light in the Lord. Live as children of light...This is why it is said: "Wake up, sleeper, rise from the dead, and Christ will shine on you." Be very careful, then, how you live - not as unwise but as wise, making the most of every opportunity, because the days are evil. Therefore, do not be foolish, but understand what the Lord's will is.*

MOVE #5: ACTIVATE ALL THE PEOPLE ON PURPOSE

SHIFT #5: FROM MORE PROGRAMS ... TO MORE MISSION FIELDS

BIG IDEA: THE CHURCH IS MADE TO GO MORE.

The people of God have already been sent and placed strategically by Jesus. Mission begins by expressing the fullness of Jesus where we live, work, study and play. Every disciple is a missionary with a unique mission field, which becomes a personal mosaic of mission. All those overlapping mosaics of mission are Jesus' plan to express His fullness into every corner of culture and into every sphere of society. Each mosaic significantly extends the "footprint of fullness." Our "GO" is to embrace our mission field and "make the most of every opportunity" to express the FULLNESS of Jesus to others.

The discussions in this study will be rich and fruitful. Stay mindful of the time as each question only has 3 to 4 minutes allotted. Fully engage the interaction with your team but be careful not to dominate the conversation. Seek first to listen, allowing others to share their thoughts. Let your thinking be stimulated, but don't feel like the tension in every question needs to be relieved.

lilADE FOR MOR⨳

LESSON 05
CONVERSATION GUIDE ▶

DISCUSSION QUESTIONS

1. Read Ephesians 5 together. What are some of your observations about Jesus and the church?

2. In lesson 1, you discussed the mystery of Jesus and the church having the capacity to fill everything in every way. If the church is to carry the fullness of Jesus into every crack and cranny of society, how will that happen?

   Can it happen with the strategy your church currently has for mobilization?

3. In Ephesians 4 and 5, Paul gives a comprehensive list of instructions for Christian living. Amidst this list of instructions, Paul says, "make the most of every opportunity." For the radically busy people with whom you minister, how is this practical?

4. What would it look like for a church focused on disciple making to see its core strategy as mobilizing everyday missionaries (on their Ephesians 2:10 calling) to unique mission fields where each person works, lives, studies and plays?

   What are the benefits of this type of approach?

   What are the obstacles to overcome?

   What would have to happen to make this a reality?

5. What stood out to you from the Lesson 5 reading, reflection questions and videos? Why?

TAMPA UNDERGROUND DOCUMENTARY *35 MINUTES*
WATCH VIDEO #15 TOGETHER AS A TEAM.

Back to the beginning...

KEY PARADIGM THOUGHT
THE KINGDOM IS BIGGER THAN THE CHURCH.

"Being a part of a community on campus that was trying to bring the Kingdom of God on earth as it is in heaven was a risk, an adventure, a time of dreaming and going from that to a space where you were only challenged to think about the Kingdom of God on Sunday morning. Really, that (the Kingdom of God) just being the Church itself, the buildings, the programs, just felt...it was a disappointment. It left me feeling empty."

> —Melyssa Cordero, Underground Tampa,
>   Minority Leadership Director

KEY PARADIGM THOUGHT
THE MINISTRY AND MISSION THAT GOD HAS GIFTED MANY OF HIS PEOPLE FOR WILL NOT FIT THE PROGRAMS OF THE CHURCH.

"I wanted to get involved. I wanted to do something! The only options that were available were singing on the worship team, kid's ministry or women's ministry. There has to be more. God is doing more in me, and it doesn't fit in the parameters of these options. Is there anything else?"

> —Kiesha Polonio, Tampa Underground, Associate Director

KEY PARADIGM THOUGHT
THE UNDERGROUND VALUES LIST.

Jesus. The poor. The lost. The whole world. Empowerment. Kingdom Mission. Micro churches. Simplicity. Culture & Ethnicity. Biblical Justice. Each Other. Contextualization. Humility. Passion. Zeal & Contemplation. The Bible. Sharing & Giving. Prayer & Dependence.

IIIADE FOR MOR⊒

LESSON 05
CONVERSATION GUIDE ▶

After watching Video #15 **(exponential.org/more)** spend time talking through the Discussion Questions as a team.

Remember, a paradigm is what you think before you think about it. You'll never experience lasting change without examining those thoughts and allowing the Word and the Spirit to transform your assumptions.

DISCUSSION QUESTIONS

1. We highlighted "Key Paradigm Thoughts." Highlight the "key paradigm" that you saw in the video story. What stood out to you?

2. How would you describe the core paradigm the Tampa Underground operates on if you had to boil things down to just ONE key paradigm?

3. What challenged and confronted you the most?

4. What encouraged and comforted you the most?

5. What tensions are you feeling? Why?

LESSON 05
MADE TO GO MORE

TEAM PERSPECTIVE	20 MINUTES
MOVE #5: ACTIVATE ALL PEOPLE ON PURPOSE	

TEAM NOTES
Have someone on your team continue the "official set of notes" with your answers to the questions in this section and in the subsequent "Shift Section." Remember, these notes will be used in Lesson 7 to develop an action plan.

BIG IDEA: JESUS IS MORE! THE CHURCH IS MADE FOR MORE! THE CHURCH IS MADE TO BE MORE! THE CHURCH IS MADE TO DO MORE! THE CHURCH IS MADE TO GO MORE!

"Our paradigm is our repeated life story that determines how an organization feels, thinks and thus acts. This system's story determines the way an organization behaves no matter how the organizational chart is drawn. The paradigm explains and then it guides behavior; and because of this, it is the primary template that shapes all other things. Restructure the organization but leave the original paradigm in place and nothing changes within the organization."

—Bill Easum, *Unfreezing Moves: Following Jesus into the Mission Field*

What's the life story of your church? What is the combination of beliefs, metaphors, origin story, hero stories, victories, tragedies, operating systems, values and daily practices that make up the story within which your church lives? That's your paradigm.

In each part of the following team conversation, you are asked to look at your context but in a new way. Although two approaches will be presented as contrasts, we fully acknowledge and celebrate the need for both! However, we're asking you to consider: "Do you embrace both approaches? Is it balanced? Are you biased to one approach?" The dynamic tension we are creating is not an attack but an opportunity to see something new.

MADE FOR MORE

LESSON 05
CONVERSATION GUIDE ▶

Remember, right now you are making a thoughtful, grace-filled and brutally honest assessment of your church, your team and your lives. You'll collect thoughts on how to apply this along the way, but you shouldn't make any decision on your future direction until your final lesson.

1. Let's go back to our Home Depot analogy from the Introduction. Take a minute and place a check mark next to each of the statements below that apply to your church (eight total).

THE "WE CAN BUILD IT. YOU CAN HELP." APPROACH FOR ACTIVATING ALL THE PEOPLE ON PURPOSE

☐ We aggressively attempt to activate all the people into the programs of the church.

☐ We sound the wake-up call for missional opportunities like short term mission trips and service in the inner city.

☐ We make heroes of our volunteers and tell their stories publicly.

☐ We try to make it as easy as possible for people to take a step toward ministry and mission.

THE "YOU CAN BUILD IT. WE CAN HELP." APPROACH FOR ACTIVATING ALL THE PEOPLE ON PURPOSE

☐ We aggressively attempt to activate all the people into every corner of culture and every sphere of society.

☐ We sound the wake-up call to a missionary identity where we live, work, study and play.

☐ We make heroes of people living out their personal calling and tell their stories publicly.

☐ We recognize that we can't save people from the discomfort and sacrifice of a missionary lifestyle, so we equip them to count the cost, live in community and care for their souls.

2. Which ones did you check? Unpack why.

3. How balanced are you between the two approaches? Which are you biased toward?

4. What percentage of your people have been awakened to their identity as everyday missionaries with unique mission fields only they can reach?

5. How well are you organized to activate people as missionaries to be on mission where they live, work, study and play?

6. What is your current scoreboard? How could it better express everyone as everyday missionaries activated in every corner of culture?

TEAM ASSESSMENT

1. How would you rate your commitment as a team to the "You Can Build It. We Can Help." approach of Activating All the People on Purpose?

2. What, if any, are the obstacles that would keep you from Activating All the People on Purpose?

PURSUING THE SHIFT: FROM MORE PROGRAMS ... TO MORE MISSION FIELDS

15 MINUTES

TEAM NOTES

Add your team's conclusions in this section into the master list highlighted in the previous section. By capturing this perspective now, you will have what's needed to develop a solid action plan in Lesson 7.

The "Shift" section is intended to build on the previous Team Perspective section and help you start the process of moving from good ideas and intentions about "organize for fullness" and shifting from "more hierarchy" to "more missionaries" into tangible action.

These six essential shifts collectively integrate to create a culture of Mobilization God's Way. In each of the six core lessons, you are looking at one shift to discern (1) where you are as a church today, (2) what mobilization in your church could look like in five years if you fully embraced the shift and (3) specific issues that would need to be addressed to make the shift successfully.

In this lesson, you are focused on the shift: FROM MORE PROGRAMS ... TO MORE MISSION FIELDS!

The following exercise and questions are not intended to finalize your actions, but it is instead meant to get you thinking toward the future and unified on some core conclusions and convictions.

DISCUSSION QUESTIONS

1. Read through the following distinctions between *more programs* and *more mission fields*. Assess where you are as a church on the spectrum of "more programs" versus "more mission fields."

LESSON 05
MADE TO GO MORE

MORE PROGRAMS MEANS...

☐ We best reach the world with great centralized programs started and maintained by the organized church.

☐ We will have the greatest impact by making sure the pastors and professionals decide what is best when it comes to impacting the community.

☐ We must streamline programs to maintain focus which will yield excellence and impact.

MORE MISSION FIELDS MEANS...

☐ We best reach the world by equipping great missionaries who start and maintain communities on mission addressing needs and making disciples in new contexts.

☐ We will have the greatest impact by allowing the Holy Spirit to lead people to what is best for the community in which He has sent them. This is encouraged and supported with coaching from their church leaders.

☐ We must streamline centralized programs to maintain focus, which will yield excellence and impact. This creates a discipleship pathway that equips and releases people to live as missionaries in their context where new ministry will emerge that we don't control.

2. Is this a shift worth the effort to pursue and to see put in place? How important is it to you? Why or why not?

IIIADE FOR MORE

3. In five years from now, if you were mobilizing God's people God's way with an approach that was rooted in "more missionaries" rather than "more hierarchy," what would that look like? What would the characteristics of success be? What benefits? Create a list of characteristics that collectively describes a preferable future.

4. What challenges and obstacles would you face?

5. What specific issues do you know would need to be addressed?

6. Are there actions you already know you'd need to take that can be identified now?

7. Are there any that you suspect are needed but require more investigation? Highlight them in your list.

LESSON 05
MADE TO GO MORE

AT THIS POINT, YOU'RE JUST COLLECTING IDEAS.
YOU SHOULDN'T MAKE ANY DECISIONS UNTIL LESSON 7.

NEXT WEEK

Next week, we move on to Ephesians 6, Move #6 and Essential Shift #6. Be sure that you have the Participant's Guide for Lesson 6 and that you understand what work is to be completed before the next gathering.

• **Read Ephesians 6 and Lesson 6.** Journal your observations.

• **Watch Video #16** (Rob Wegner and Randy Frazee on Ephesians 6).

• **Watch Video #17** (Case Study of Gateway Church).

CLOSING PRAYER

MADE FOR MORE

LESSON 06

2019

VIDEOS CAN BE ACCESSED AT
EXPONENTIAL.ORG/MORE

MADE TO WIN MORE

SCRIPTURE - EPHESIANS 6

Ephesians 6:10-12
Finally, be strong in the Lord and in his mighty power. Put on the full armor of God, so that you can take your stand against the devil's schemes. For our struggle is not against flesh and blood, but against the rulers, against the authorities, against the powers of this dark world and against the spiritual forces of evil in the heavenly realms

MOVE #6: PREPARE FOR BATTLE

SHIFT #6: FROM MORE STRATEGY ... TO MORE SURRENDER

BIG IDEA: THE CHURCH IS MADE TO WIN MORE.

The Enemy will do everything possible to thwart God's plan for More, mobilizing God's people God's way, as described in Ephesians. But in Christ, we are called to win this battle. To do so, we must consecrate ourselves for Jesus and His mission. Individually, the enemy will attempt to hinder the fullness in us, restricting the expression of this fullness carried to others. Corporately, when Paul speaks of "principalities and powers," this is another way of saying systems of oppression influenced by the demonic. Often these systems are operating INSIDE the church.

Pathway: This lesson consists of approximately one hour of advance preparation work for team members and a 75 to 90-minute interactive group gathering.

LESSON 06
MADE TO WIN MORE

PREPARATION BEFORE TEAM GATHERING

- Read Ephesians 6 and answer reflection questions. (10 minutes)

- Watch Video #16 – Rob Wegner and Randy Frazee on Ephesians 6 (25 minutes) and fill in the answers.

- Read Lesson 6 and complete the discussion questions. (25 minutes)

  - Reflect on and answer the Introduction Discussion Questions.

  - Complete the questions in the church, team and personal assessment sections. These questions will be used for a rich conversation among team members during the team gathering. Be sure to invest time working through these assessment questions.

- Prayer – Spend some time praying for this week's team meeting.

TEAM GATHERING

- Read Ephesians 6 together. (5 minutes)

- Discuss Introduction questions. (10 minutes)

- Watch Video #17 – Case Study of Gateway Church (25 minutes) and write down at least one observation that captured your thinking in the space below.

- Discuss Video #17 and Key Paradigm Thoughts. (10 minutes)

- Team Perspective and Assessment – Discuss assessment questions. (20 minutes)

- Shift #6 discussion and action. (15 minutes)

- Preview Lesson 7 expectations and prayer. (5 minutes)

INDIVIDUAL
PREPARATION

LESSON 06 ▸
INDIVIDUAL PREP

1. Read Ephesians 6. Like the previous lesson, pretend you've never experienced church and that what you read in Ephesians 6 is your first and only exposure to the characteristics of church. What conclusions or assumptions would you make about church?

2. If your church were to change the way it mobilizes God's people based on what you've been learning in this study, how large of a "battle" would you face? Would the changes be evolutionary and relatively minor OR would they be revolutionary and large?

3. What emotions (e.g. fear, uncertainty, etc.) have you felt throughout this study that Satan might be using to hold you captive?

4. What, in particular, about the passage convicted you personally about something in your life and leadership?

ROB WEGNER & RANDY FRAZEE   *15 MINUTES*
ON EPHESIANS 6
COMPLETE THE FOLLOWING AS YOU WATCH VIDEO #16.

EPHESIANS 6: ROB WEGNER

Ephesians 6:10-12
Finally, be strong in the Lord and in his mighty power. Put on the full armor of God, so that you can take your stand against the devil's schemes. For our struggle is not against flesh and blood, but against the rulers, against the authorities, against the powers of this dark world and against the spiritual forces of evil in the heavenly realms.

BIG IDEA: THE CHURCH IS MADE TO WIN MORE.

The Enemy will do everything possible to thwart God's plan for More, mobilizing God's people God's way, as describe in Ephesians. But in Christ, we are called to win this battle. To do so, we must consecrate ourselves for Jesus and His mission. Individually, the enemy will attempt to hinder the fullness in us, restricting the expression of this fullness carried to others. Corporately, when Paul speaks of "principalities and powers," this is another way of saying systems of oppression influenced by the demonic. Often these systems are operating INSIDE the church.

MOVE #6: PREPARE FOR BATTLE

The battle is not just out there; it is_____here (the mind).

The battle in the desert temptation wasn't just at the activity level but at

the_____level.

Some demonic systems have penetrated the church. For example, the

clergy and laity divide is a demonic_____system.

ꟾꟾADE FOR MORꟾ

THE ARMOR OF GOD: RANDY FRAZEE

The book of Ephesians contains the famous Armor of God description and is not written to an individual but rather to the_____of believers.

We need to reframe the armor in this_____sense, an_____unbroken circle of God's people walking arm in arm.

The belt of truth is defined by a community of believers speaking the truth in_____.

The breastplate of righteousness is shown as a community of believers, arm in arm, acting_____toward one another.

The feet fitted with the readiness that comes from the gospel of peace is perceived as the relational_____with one another.

Ephesians 2:14
For he himself is our peace, who has made the two groups one and has destroyed the barrier, the dividing wall of hostility.

The Shield of Faith is demonstrated when faith is

a_____.

When we as a community act in faith towards God and each other and when we stand arm in arm together and demonstrate faithfulness and loyalty to each other, it acts as a_____to deflect the fiery arrow of the enemy.

The last two pieces of the armor are_____.

The Sword of the Spirit is demonstrated when the Word is not just a noun, it is a_____.

Pray in the Spirit is shown when the community of believers engages together in God's Word and prays for guidance in their lives. It provides the best_____strategy to ward off the attacks of the evil one.

LESSON 06
INDIVIDUAL PREP ▶

Review the Lesson 6 content from the past few pages (The Key Verses, the Move, the Shift, the Big Idea, your Notes from Ephesians and the Teaching Video Notes) and complete the following:

1. What stood out to you from the Lesson 6 reading material and videos? Why?

2. Flip forward to the Conversation Guide section, review the questions in the church and team assessment inside the lesson. These questions will be used for deeper conversations among team members during the team gathering. Be sure to invest time reflecting on these assessment questions.

3. How well are you living out your identity in Christ?

4. To what degree are you practicing "offensive" prayer against the demonic?

5. How intentional are you in consecrating for battle?

6. Spend some time praying.

CONVERSATION
GUIDE

LESSON 06
CONVERSATION GUIDE

INTRODUCTION AND REFLECTION   *20 MINUTES*

Today we will jump into Ephesians 6.

> **Ephesians 6:10-12**
> *Finally, be strong in the Lord and in his mighty power. Put on the full armor of God, so that you can take your stand against the devil's schemes. For our struggle is not against flesh and blood, but against the rulers, against the authorities, against the powers of this dark world and against the spiritual forces of evil in the heavenly realms.*

MOVE #6: PREPARE FOR BATTLE

SHIFT #6: FROM MORE STRATEGY …
TO MORE SURRENDER

BIG IDEA: THE CHURCH IS MADE TO WIN MORE.

The Enemy will do everything possible to thwart God's plan for More, mobilizing God's people, God's way, as describe in Ephesians. But in Christ, we are called to win this battle. To do so, we must consecrate ourselves for Jesus and His mission. Individually, the enemy will attempt to hinder the fullness in us, restricting the expression of this fullness carried to others. Corporately, when Paul speaks of "principalities and powers," this is another way of saying systems of oppression influenced by the demonic. Often these systems are operating INSIDE the church.

The discussions in this study will be rich and fruitful. Stay mindful of the time, as each question only has three to four minutes allotted. Fully engage the interaction with your team, but be careful not to dominate the conversation. Seek first to listen, allowing others to share their thoughts. Let your thinking be stimulated, but don't feel like the tension in every question needs to be relieved.

LESSON 06
MADE TO WIN MORE ▶

1. Read Ephesians 6 together. What are some of your observations about Jesus and the church?

2. In what ways might your current approach to mobilization hold you captive?

3. If making changes in the way you mobilize God's people is a "preparation for battle," what obstacles might you expect?

   What do you need to do to prepare?

4. What stood out to you from the Lesson 6 reading, reflection questions and videos? Why?

CASE STUDY OF GATEWAY CHURCH   *25 MINUTES*
WATCH VIDEO #17 TOGETHER AS A TEAM.

IIIADE FOR MOR≡

LESSON 06
CONVERSATION GUIDE ▶

After watching Video #17, spend time talking through the Discussion Questions as a team.

Remember, a paradigm is what you think before you think about it. You'll never experience lasting change without examining those thoughts and allowing the Word and the Spirit to transform your assumptions.

Here are some key paradigm shifting ideas from the case study of Gateway Church. Read through these as a team.

KEY PARADIGM THOUGHT
SPIRIT-EMPOWERED HEALING FOR WOUNDEDNESS AND FREEDOM FROM CAPTIVITY ARE ESSENTIAL IN THE BEGINNING OF DISCIPLESHIP.

Gateway church exists to see people saved, healed, set free, discipled, equipped, empowered and serving. It's a process statement. It's a discipleship statement. In our experience, Spirit-empowered freedom from captivity and healing for woundedness are essential to the beginning of discipleship. Many churches are missing the healing and freedom components in discipleship. These two steps are a necessary bridge for most people to cross over into deeper discipleship.

KEY PARADIGM THOUGHT
REST IS THE GREATEST NEED FOR MOST PEOPLE IN A CULTURE OBSESSED WITH BUSYNESS.

We want to minister out of a place of rest, of knowing deeply our identity in Christ. Healing and Freedom Ministries are essential to restoring a gospel-centered identity in people's souls, so they can work from a place of rest. Otherwise, the Church and its programs just add to the sense of busyness and fatigue in their lives.

LESSON 06
MADE TO WIN MORE ▶

KEY PARADIGM THOUGHT
FREEDOM STARTS WITH THE LEADER. YOU CAN'T GIVE AWAY WHAT YOU HAVEN'T RECEIVED.

The first step of the church finding freedom is the church's leaders finding freedom in Christ. Each of those leaders needs to create a safe place to hear God. We need to learn how to "sit down" inside of ourselves and learn to receive from God. Prayer is not a monologue but a dialogue. Silence and stillness are necessary for us to find freedom in Christ.

KEY PARADIGM THOUGHT
NORMALIZE THE NEED FOR FREEDOM.

Create a culture of freedom where seeking freedom from areas of captivity is not stigmatized but celebrated. Admit, especially at the leadership level, we are "messed up." We all have permission to admit that, but we don't have permission to remain there. Create a "freedom pathway" where people know the vehicles they can ride in toward freedom. This can include classes and seminars that build to retreats (Kairos). The classes include times of individual counseling and prayer. On the back side of Kairos, many no longer seek or need one on one counseling. Beyond Kairos, freedom groups exist according to certain themes or needs.

DISCUSSION QUESTIONS FROM THE GATEWAY CHURCH VIDEO

1. What challenged and confronted you the most?

2. What encouraged and comforted you the most?

3. What tensions are you feeling? Why?

MADE FOR MORE _____

LESSON 06
CONVERSATION GUIDE

TEAM NOTES

Have someone on your team continue the "official set of notes" with your answers to the questions in this section and in the subsequent "Shift Section." These notes will be very helpful to you in Lesson 7.

BIG IDEA: JESUS IS MORE! THE CHURCH IS MADE *FOR* MORE! THE CHURCH IS MADE *TO BE* MORE! THE CHURCH IS MADE TO *DO* MORE! THE CHURCH IS MADE TO *GO* MORE! THE CHURCH IS MADE TO *WIN* MORE!

Remember, a paradigm is what we think before we think about it. At this point in the journey, we hope you've done some heavy thinking about what you think before you think.

MOVE #6: PREPARE FOR BATTLE

In each part of the following team conversation, you are asked to look at your context but in a new way. Although two approaches will be presented as contrasts, we fully acknowledge and celebrate the need for both! However, we're asking you to consider: "Do you embrace both approaches? Is it balanced? Are you biased to one approach?" The dynamic tension we are creating is not an attack, but an opportunity to see something new.

LESSON 06
MADE TO WIN MORE

CHURCH ASSESSMENT

Remember, right now you are making a thoughtful, grace-filled and brutally honest assessment of your church, your team and your lives. You'll collect thoughts on how to apply this along the way, but you shouldn't make any decision on your future direction until your final lesson.

1. Let's go back to our Home Depot analogy from the Introduction. Take a minute and place a check mark next to each of the statements below that apply to your church (ten total).

THE "WE CAN BUILD IT. YOU CAN HELP." APPROACH FOR PREPARING FOR BATTLE

☐ We understand that most people see church as a building, an event or a program.

☐ We understand the church needs professionals the people can depend on to minister to them.

☐ We understand that people have temptations, and we equip them to say,"No!"

☐ We understand we need to pray regularly against the attacks of the enemy.

☐ We understand each of us must fight the battle against the enemy.

THE "YOU CAN BUILD IT. WE CAN HELP." APPROACH FOR PREPARING FOR BATTLE

☐ We regularly declare and train our people to understand that the church is not a building; it's a body. The church is not driven by events but by an everyday mission in all of life. The church is not a program but the people of God. We recognize that language builds culture, so we are careful to communicate that "you can't go to Church, you can only be the Church." We understand that accepting the "normal definition" of Church is actually giving ground to the enemy.

☐ We understand the clergy/laity divide is the perpetuation of the old covenant at best and the continuation of pagan thinking at worst. As elders and leaders in the church, we recognize our success is measured by how successfully we equip all the people of God to minister and be on mission.

IIIADE FOR MORƎ

☐ We understand the real battle in every temptation is not at the activity level but at the identity level. Only through a biblically-shaped, spirit-empowered healing of our image of God and our self-identity can we win the battle against temptation.

☐ We understand the gates of Hell will not prevail against us. We are on the offense in strategic prayer and the prophetic use of the Word of God in teaching and equipping.

☐ We understand that we can only win this battle together as a body!

2. Which ones did you check? Unpack why.

3. How balanced are you between the two approaches? Which are you biased toward?

4. What percentage of your people settle for a "go to Church" mentality?

How are you addressing it?

5. What percentage of your people accept or even celebrate the clergy/laity divide? How are you addressing it?

6. How are you strategically addressing the healing of people's image of God and helping them discover and live in their identity in Christ?

7. How are you on the offense through prayer and the Word? How are you bringing the body together to win the battle?

LESSON 06
MADE TO WIN MORE ▶

1. How would you rate your commitment as a team to the "You Can Build It. We Can Help." approach of Preparing for Battle?

2. What, if any, are the obstacles that would keep you from Preparing for Battle?

PURSUING THE SHIFT: FROM MORE STRATEGY ... TO MORE SURRENDER
15 MINUTES

TEAM NOTES
Add your team's conclusions in this section into the master list highlighted in the previous section. By capturing this perspective now, you will have what's needed to develop a solid action plan in the next lesson.

The "Shift" section is intended to build on the previous Team Perspective section and help you start the process of moving from good ideas and intentions about "preparing for battle" and shifting from "more strategy" to "more surrender" into tangible action.

**In this lesson, you are focused on the shift:
FROM MORE STRATEGY ... TO MORE SURRENDER!**

The following exercise and questions are meant to get you thinking toward the future and unified on some core conclusions and convictions. For now, don't be limited by what you think you can and cannot do. Instead dream about a future in which this shift becomes a reality.

IIIADE FOR MOR≡

LESSON 06
CONVERSATION GUIDE

DISCUSSION QUESTIONS

1. Read through the following distinctions between more programs and more mission fields. Assess where you are as a church on the spectrum of "more programs" versus "more mission fields."

MORE STRATEGY MEANS...

☐ We plug people into our discipleship strategy as quickly as we can. Those who need extra grace can seek out counseling.

☐ We plan and pray for God to grant success to the plan.

☐ We understand that any strategy is going to be difficult to enact, so we work hard to work the plan.

MORE SURRENDER MEANS...

☐ We plug people into their identity in Christ, a sense of rest in the Gospel, healing from woundedness and freedom from captivity. This is essential to the beginning stages of discipleship for all people.

☐ We pray and seek to discern what the Spirit is saying to our community. All planning stems from listening to the Spirit and is sustained through prayer.

☐ We understand we are in a spiritual battle with principalities and powers that we will not be able to beat through merely human efforts producing merely human results. We actively use the armor of God as a community to win this spiritual battle.

2. Is this a shift that is worth the effort to pursue and to see put in place? How important is it to you? Why or why not?

3. In five years from now, if you were mobilizing God's people, God's way with an approach that was rooted in "more surrender" rather than "more strategy," what would that look like? What would the characteristics of success be? What benefits? Create a list of characteristics that collectively describes a preferable future.

4. What challenges and obstacles would you face?

5. What specific issues do you know would need to be addressed?

6. Are there actions you already know you'd need to take that can be identified now?

7. Are there any that you suspect are needed but require more investigation? Highlight them in your list.

LESSON 06
CONVERSATION GUIDE ▶

NEXT WEEK

Next week, we pull together all that we've learned into an integrated list and draw conclusions. We will look back at our conversations from Lessons 1 through 6 and seek to identify the things we need to change. We will develop a list of "What's Important Now" (WINS) prioritized actions together as a team.

To prepare:

• Read Ephesians 1 - 6 and journal your observations.

• Look back at your notes from previous lessons, and create a consolidated list of personal takeaways, learnings and things you'd like to change in your own life and leadership based on this study.

CLOSING PRAYER

MADE FOR MORE

LESSON 07

2019

VIDEOS CAN BE ACCESSED AT
EXPONENTIAL.ORG/MORE

As a part of equipping your team,
Exponential has 9 events coming in 2019.

MADE FOR MORE:
MOBILIZING GOD'S PEOPLE, GOD'S WAY

2019 National Event
March 4 – 7, 2019 | Orlando, FL

2019 Regional Events
Washington DC, Southern CA, Bay Area CA,
Chicago, Houston and New York City

For more information, please go to:
exponential.org/events

BEYOND GOOD INTENTIONS

INTRODUCTION AND EXPECTATIONS   *10 MINUTES*

Today, we will jump into our final lesson of the Made for More study. It's been a challenging and thought-provoking journey. Hopefully, it has caused each of you to reflect on your own values as well as the corporate culture you've collectively created.

It's time to turn your sights on the future and unify your team on steps forward. What kind of mobilization culture do you dream of in three to five years?

Today's lesson is all about being intentional to unify as a team on where you've been, where you are today, where you'd like to be in three to five years and what specific steps are needed in the coming months to give you some momentum and move you in the right direction. You can't change everything overnight. You must be patient but intentional.

You will seek to take what you've covered previously and develop a simple list of "What's Important Now" actions. You will NOT be creating a final, comprehensive action plan for achieving a new five-year vision and culture for mobilization. Instead, you will identify the next, vital steps needed to move you forward in the right direction.

In this lesson, you will:

1. Review the six shifts and six moves from Ephesians 1 – 6.

2. Look back at your team assessments and acquired knowledge from the six moves and six shifts seeking to have a unified understanding of your church's current strengths and weaknesses in mobilizing God's people, God's way.

3. Complete a summary assessment of where you see your church on each of the six moves and shifts, seeking to bring clarity to the gaps between where you are and where you'd like to be in the full maturity of each shift.

4. Consider the scope of change required and the possible pathways for moving forward.

5. Identify key next steps in each of the six moves and shifts to give forward momentum in the right direction.

LESSON 07
BEYOND GOOD INTENTIONS

1. What has the Holy Spirit been whispering (or shouting) to you throughout this study?

2. What emotion best characterizes how you are feeling about what you've covered in this study?

3. What has you most excited about what you've learned in this study?

4. What has you most concerned?

IIIADE FOR MORᴲ

LESSON 07
BEYOND GOOD INTENTIONS

GUT CHECK

Before moving on, pause and see if there is consensus on the scope of changes you need to make and the relative importance of this as a top priority.

DISCUSSION QUESTIONS   *30 MINUTES*

1. Rate you church on a scale of 1 to 10. Base this on 1 being defined as a volunteer mobilization effort driven by "filling slots" that keeps critical programs operating. Define 10 as a "calling-based" mobilization where each person is considered an everyday missionary called to a unique mission field where he or she lives, works and plays (Ephesians 2:10).

2. How important is it that you move this toward a 10 if you're not already there?

3. How significant of a change effort would this be compared to other change initiatives the church has undertaken?

4. Does this rise to the level of importance to make it a critical, church-wide, strategic initiative?

LESSON 07
BEYOND GOOD INTENTIONS

*"People in any organization are always attached to the obsolete -
the things that should have worked but did not, the things that once
were productive and no longer are."*
 —Peter Drucker

5. Are there things you are holding onto as a church that are obsolete
   or no longer productive, and you would have to let go of to create a
   culture of mobilization? What things?

6. Peter Drucker, the father of modern management said, "Results are
   obtained by exploiting opportunities, not by solving problems." All
   problems can be reframed into opportunities. Brainstorm a list of what
   problems you would be solving by seeking to transform your culture of
   mobilization:

Now, attempt to reframe this list of problems into a single, compelling
opportunity statement:

IIIADE FOR MORΞ

7. Which of the three pathways best describe the one you would likely need to take:

a. **"Revolutionary Change" (a System Reset)** – This is a major overhaul and change to your operating system for mobilizing everyday missionaries to their unique mission fields where they work, live and play. This would also be the most likely path for a brand-new church.

b. **"Evolutionary Change" (Incremental Change)** – This is an integrated plan to make incremental changes across most ministries with the collective impact being a shift in your overall culture. The results of this type of change are meaningful but likely to fall short of "revolutionary change" where the entire operating system is reset.

c. **"Research and Development" (Limited Scope Revolutionary Change)** Instead of doing a system reset across the entire church all at once, this path selects one to three ministries (new or existing) on which to run pilots. An entire "reset" would be done to the operating system within that specific ministry.

LESS AND MORE   *30 MINUTES*

NOTE:
Your team should have kept integrated team notes from the team assessment and shift sections per the instructions in each of the first six lessons. Hopefully, these were comprehensive and a collective representation of your team. Be sure everyone has a printed copy of those integrated notes for the remainder of this lesson.

The six shifts represent a movement from one type of behavior to another. We need LESS of one thing and MORE of another. In the following exercise, brainstorm a list of characteristics of what "LESS" and "MORE" would look like in your context for each of the six shifts.

REVIEW OF EPHESIANS 1 – MADE FOR MORE

KEY PASSAGE:

Ephesians 1:22-23
And God placed all things under his feet and appointed him to be head over everything for the church, which is his body, the fullness of him who fills everything in every way.

CRITICAL MOVE #1: ILLUMINATE THE MYSTERY

ESSENTIAL SHIFT #1: FROM MORE EFFORT ... TO MORE JESUS

DISCUSSION QUESTIONS

1. On a scale of 1 to 10, where does your current culture of mobilization fall?

```
MORE                                                           MORE
EFFORT  ├───┼───┼───┼───┼───┼───┼───┼───┼───┤                  JESUS
        1   2   3   4   5   6   7   8   9   10
```

LESSON 07
BEYOND GOOD INTENTIONS ▶

2. So, we want a culture of mobilization that is represented by "less effort" and "more Jesus." Henry Blackaby talks about how we want to cooperate with God where He is already at work. We want to help people discover the unique, Ephesians 2:10, personal calling; and then, we want to mobilize them as everyday missionaries to their unique mission fields in all corners of our community. At first glance that could feel like "more effort," but let's assume it's not. If we had a culture of mobilization in place that did require "less effort" and "more Jesus," what would that look like in our context? Use the space below to identify specific behaviors, values and priorities we would need to embrace.

LESS EFFORT:

MORE JESUS:

LESSON 07
BEYOND GOOD INTENTIONS

KEY PASSAGE:

Ephesians 2:8-10
For it is by grace you have been saved, through faith - and this is not from yourselves, it is the gift of God - not by works, so that no one can boast. For we are God's handiwork, created in Christ Jesus to do good works, which God prepared in advance for us to do...

CRITICAL MOVE #2: INVESTIGATE THE DESIGN

ESSENTIAL SHIFT #2: FROM MORE VOLUNTEERS ... TO MORE MASTERPIECES (AND MISSIONARIES)

DISCUSSION QUESTIONS

1. On a scale of 1 to 10, where does your current culture of mobilization fall?

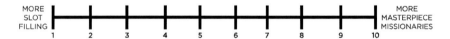

MORE SLOT FILLING | 1   2   3   4   5   6   7   8   9   10 | MORE MASTERPIECE MISSIONARIES

IIIADE FOR MORE

2. We want a culture of mobilization that is represented by "less volunteers" simply filling slots and "more masterpieces" serving as missionaries within their unique calling. We want a process in place that sees each follower of Jesus as a unique masterpiece with a unique part to play in God's plan. If we had a culture of mobilization in place that did require "less slot filling" and "more mobilized missionaries," what would that look like in our context? Use the space below to identify specific behaviors, values and priorities we would need to embrace.

LESS SLOT FILLING:

MORE MASTERPIECE MISSIONARIES:

LESSON 07
BEYOND GOOD INTENTIONS ▶

KEY PASSAGE:

Ephesians 3:16-21
I pray that out of his glorious riches he may strengthen you with power through his Spirit in your inner being, so that Christ may dwell in your hearts through faith. And I pray that you, being rooted and established in love, may have power, together with all the Lord's holy people, to grasp how wide and long and high and deep is the love of Christ, and to know this love that surpasses knowledge - that you may be filled to the measure of all the fullness of God. Now to him who is able to do immeasurably more than all we ask or imagine, according to his power that is at work within us, to him be glory in the church and in Christ Jesus throughout all generations, for ever and ever! Amen.

CRITICAL MOVE #3: MOTIVATE WITH LOVE

ESSENTIAL SHIFT #3: FROM MORE GUILT ... TO MORE LOVE

DISCUSSION QUESTIONS

1. On a scale of 1 to 10, where does your current culture of mobilization fall?

MORE GUILT   1   2   3   4   5   6   7   8   9   10   MORE LOVE

2. We want a culture of mobilization that is represented by "less guilting" of volunteers and "more love" motivation by genuinely wanting to help people discover and deploy their God-given, unique sweet-spot of personal calling. We want a process in place that unifies everyone on our common or general calling to be disciples who make disciples wherever we are. We want this process to then value the unique, personal calling of each believer and his or her unique role in the primary mission. We want pure motives to drive our process as we

IIIADE FOR MORᴇ

LESSON 07
BEYOND GOOD INTENTIONS ▶

embrace the truth that discipleship in its purest sense helps others discover the unique calling Jesus has given each person. If we had a culture of mobilization in place that did require "less guilting" and "more pure discipleship motives," what would that look like in our context? Use the space below to identify specific behaviors, values and priorities we would need to embrace.

LESS GUILT:

MORE LOVE (PURE AND RIGHT MOTIVES):

LESSON 07
BEYOND GOOD INTENTIONS ▶

REVIEW OF EPHESIANS 4 – MADE TO DO MORE

KEY PASSAGE:

Ephesians 4:11-16
So, Christ himself gave the apostles, the prophets, the evangelists, the pastors and teachers, to equip his people for works of service, so that the body of Christ may be built up until we all reach unity in the faith and in the knowledge of the Son of God and become mature, attaining to the whole measure of the fullness of Christ. Then we will no longer be infants, tossed back and forth by the waves, and blown here and there by every wind of teaching and by the cunning and craftiness of people in their deceitful scheming. Instead, speaking the truth in love, we will grow to become in every respect the mature body of him who is the head, that is, Christ. From him the whole body, joined and held together by every supporting ligament, grows and builds itself up in love, as each part does its work.

CRITICAL MOVE #4: ORGANIZE FOR FULLNESS

ESSENTIAL SHIFT #4: FROM MORE HIERARCHY ...
TO MORE MISSIONARIES

DISCUSSION QUESTIONS

1. On a scale of 1 to 10, where does your current culture of mobilization fall?

MORE HIERARCHY & STRUCTURE | 1 2 3 4 5 6 7 8 9 10 | MORE MISSIONARIES & FULLNESS

2. We want a culture of mobilization that is represented by "less hierarchy, structure and clergy/laity divide" and "more missionaries" deployed on their God-given, unique sweet-spot of personal calling to carry the fullness of Jesus into every nook and cranny of society. We want a process that values "yes" and is "permission giving." We want this process to value the principle of "You can do it. We can help." We want to see the church as a home base and a launching pad for everyday missionaries deployed to their unique corners of society. We want to value the mosaic of gifts given

IIIADE FOR MORΞ

by Jesus to his people and to see these gifts as our primary means of equipping for mobilizing everyday missionaries. We want to embrace the truth that the church will not reach its full potential and maturity if just one disciple fails to embrace his or her unique gifts. We want to limit as much bureaucracy as possible that inhibits the deploying of an army of everyday missionaries. If we had a culture of mobilization in place that did require "less hierarchy, structure and clergy/laity divide" and "more missionaries" deployed, what would that look like in our context? Use the space below to identify specific behaviors, values and priorities we would need to embrace.

LESS HIERARCHY AND STRUCTURE:

MORE MISSIONARIES AND FULLNESS:

LESSON 07
BEYOND GOOD INTENTIONS ▶

KEY PASSAGE:

Ephesians 5:8, 14-17
For you were once darkness, but now you are light in the Lord. Live as children of light...This is why it is said: "Wake up, sleeper, rise from the dead, and Christ will shine on you." Be very careful, then, how you live - not as unwise but as wise, making the most of every opportunity, because the days are evil. Therefore, do not be foolish, but understand what the Lord's will is.

CRITICAL MOVE #5: ACTIVATE ON PURPOSE

ESSENTIAL SHIFT #5: FROM MORE PROGRAMS ... TO MORE MISSION FIELDS

DISCUSSION QUESTIONS

1. On a scale of 1 to 10, where does your current culture of mobilization fall?

MORE PROGRAMS   1   2   3   4   5   6   7   8   9   10   MORE MISSION FIELDS

LESSON 07
BEYOND GOOD INTENTIONS

2. We want a culture of mobilization that is represented by "less programs" to operate internally and "more mission fields" to deploy everyday missionaries. We want a process that values what happens in every nook and cranny of society where people live, work, study and play as much as it values our own internal, sacred space. We want a process that puts at least equal emphasis on the "go and be" as it does on the "come and see." If we had a culture of mobilization in place that did require "less programs" to operate and "more mission fields" to fill, what specific behaviors, values and priorities would we need to embrace?

LESS PROGRAMS:

MORE MISSION FIELDS:

REVIEW OF EPHESIANS 6 - MADE TO WIN MORE

KEY PASSAGE:

Ephesians 6:10-12
Finally, be strong in the Lord and in his mighty power. Put on the full armor of God, so that you can take your stand against the devil's schemes. For our struggle is not against flesh and blood, but against the rulers, against the authorities, against the powers of this dark world and against the spiritual forces of evil in the heavenly realms.

CRITICAL MOVE #6: PREPARE FOR BATTLE

ESSENTIAL SHIFT #6: FROM MORE STRATEGY ... TO MORE SURRENDER

DISCUSSION QUESTIONS

1. On a scale of 1 to 10, where does your current culture of mobilization fall?

MORE STRATEGY   1   2   3   4   5   6   7   8   9   10   MORE SURRENDER

2. We want a culture of mobilization that is represented by "less complex strategies" to manage and "more surrendered trust." We want a process that is simple, clear and easy for anyone to understand. We want a process that relies more heavily on prayer and the power of the Holy Spirit to intervene than on one which is controlled with human efforts. In addition, we recognize that discipleship must involve the healing and freedom only the gospel and our identity in Christ can give. We acknowledge that such a process as this (and as described in prior shifts) will bring out the worst in our enemy, Satan. We must

be prepared for the battle he will wage against us, especially when we begin to mobilize God's people, God's way. The enemy knows the impact of just one follower of Christ mobilized on his or her Ephesians 2:10 calling. Our efforts to mobilize an army of such missionaries will be met with resistance. We must be prepared for battle. If we had a culture of mobilization in place that did require "less strategy" to manage and "more surrendered trust" to God, what specific behaviors, values and priorities would we need to embrace?

LESS STRATEGY:

MORE SURRENDER:

LESSON 07
BEYOND GOOD INTENTIONS ▶

MINIMUM STAVES — *30 MINUTES*

Take some time now to pull your team's collective assessment from the previous section into perspective. For this exercise, you will use the principle of "minimum stave." Staves are the individual pieces that make up the sides of an old, wooden bucket. Now imagine each stave having a different height. Some are very short (possibly half the height of the bucket) and others are full height.

The principle of "minimum stave" says that you can only fill the bucket to the height of the shortest stave where water will leak. The shortest stave will always limit the amount of water the bucket can hold. No matter how strong and tall the other staves are, the one with the minimum height will limit your ability to fill the bucket to the top.

In a similar way, each of the six moves and shifts are like staves. You might be really strong at four of the six, but the other two will limit our effectiveness. While it's important to be aware of your minimum staves, you ultimately need to get all of them to full height.

The minimum stave exercise simply helps you put perspective on which ones are relative strengths and which are relative weaknesses. Assume each of the six shifts as discussed in the previous section are a stave. Using the assessment numbers from the previous lesson (the 1 through 10 rating your team landed on for each shift), simply fill the correct number into the first column of the table below.

In practice and in your unique church context, not all shifts are equally important at a given time. You need to be careful simply putting too much effort into your weakest shift if there are more important shifts needing priority action. Look through the list of shifts. Consider their relative importance in your setting. Give each of the six shifts a relative importance score in the second column of the table below. Rate this as 1 is the least important, and 10 is most important.

You may also want to consider whether there are any "low hanging fruit" amongst your minimums. Are there specific shifts that could produce strong improvements with minimal investment of resources? If so, you may want to give these higher Team Importance to help create some quick wins and momentum.

 IIIADE FOR MORE

LESSON 07
BEYOND GOOD INTENTIONS

Finally, using your answers in the first two columns, seek a team consensus on assigning a priority/urgency to each of the six shifts (last column of the table below).

SHIFT	TEAM RATING (1 TO 10)	TEAM IMPORTANCE (1 TO 10)	PRIORITY/URGENCY (LOW, MEDIUM, HIGH)
MORE EFFORT TO MORE JESUS			
MORE VOLUNTEERS TO MORE MASTERPIECES			
MORE GUILT TO MORE LOVE			
MORE HIERARCHY TO MORE MISSIONARIES			
MORE PROGRAMS TO MORE MISSION FIELDS			
MORE STRATEGY TO MORE SURRENDER			

WHAT'S IMPORTANT NOW?   *60 - 120 MINUTES*

You've arrived. You might say, "this is where the rubber meets the road!" You've covered a lot of ground; and hopefully, you are ready to turn your ideas and good intentions into a plan. In this exercise, you will brainstorm together a list of priority actions needed to move you forward in the right direction.

You are not creating a comprehensive, implementation plan. That comes later. Instead, this exercise seeks to orient your team compass in the right direction and give you a map to reach your first milestone on your journey.

RESOURCE KIT

Lesson 7

LESSON 07
BEYOND GOOD INTENTIONS

ACTIONS

Use large post-it notes or whiteboards for this exercise. You will need the equivalent of a few large post-it notes for each shift (at least three post-it note sheets per shift).

1. Label the first sheet "More Effort … to More Jesus"

2. Pick a date at three years into the future. Write "On [fill-in your date} our culture of mobilization will include" under the title.

3. Look back at your list of "LESS" and "MORE" for this shift. Brainstorm a list of positive characteristics and descriptors (one to five-word descriptors) by which you want your mobilization culture for this shift to be characterized. Try to brainstorm at least 10 to 15 descriptors. The collection of these descriptors should bring a compelling color picture of the future into sight. Use as many sheets as necessary to list your descriptors for this shift.

4. As a team, discuss whether you are unified on this description. When there is unity, move to the next step.

5. Repeat steps #1 and #2 on a blank sheet of paper.

6. Make a list of three specific actions you'd need to take in the next three to six months to put your team on the right path to accomplishing the vision described in step #4 above. Avoid the temptation to list more actions. Pick the three most critical actions that will enable a list of additional more detailed actions to be created in the future. Often these three critical actions include at least one or two actions that require further investigation and research with some kind of findings reported. It's this investigative work that often opens up future breakthrough thinking and action. You will likely end up with at least one action in each of the six shift areas that involves further research/investigation.

7. After brainstorming the list in #6 above, seek unity as a team on the three to five most important actions.

8. Repeat steps #1 – #7 for each shift. This should produce a list of 15 to 20 actions.

9. Spend some time praying as a team and affirming these actions as your next steps.

 IIIADE FOR MOR≡

LESSON 07
BEYOND GOOD INTENTIONS ▶

"Plans are only good intentions unless they immediately degenerate into hard work. Unless commitment is made, there are only promises and hopes... but no plans."
—Peter Drucker

Before ending your time together, take a few minutes to look back through your "What's Important Now" (WINS) list. You should have 10 to 20 specific priorities or actions. Some of these you will need to clarify through more investigation.

In looking back through each priority or action, verify that it is clear and concrete. Would 10 of 10 people who read the action, but were not involved in developing the list, know what it means? Is it written clear enough that your entire team knows exactly what it means to complete the action? Clarify the actions as needed.

Also take a few minutes to identify "who" by name has the lead on each priority/action and "when" the action is due to be completed.

A lead person should be assigned for keeping track of all the actions and

periodically reporting status updates to the team. It's also strongly encouraged that you schedule regular follow-up lessons to adjust the plan, pray, celebrate wins and share struggles.

Many of the initial actions are likely "investigation" endeavors to get answers to questions or to prioritize options. This initial round of activity will position your team well for a follow-up planning lesson to develop a more detailed and comprehensive plan.

Following through with this action list will put you on the path to developing a culture for Mobilizing God's People, God's Way!

ADDITIONAL
RESOURCES

2019

VIDEOS CAN BE ACCESSED AT
EXPONENTIAL.ORG/MORE

ADDITIONAL RESOURCES

Lesson One: Made for More: Illuminate the Mystery

Gospel Fluency: Speaking the Truths of Jesus Into the Everyday Stuff of Life by Jeff Vanderstelt and Jackie Hill Perry
gospelfluency.com

Lesson Two: Made to BE More: Investigate the Design

More: Find Your Personal Calling and Live Life to the Fullest Measure by Todd Wilson

More provides an easy-to-use framework that equips individuals to embark on a journey of discovering their unique personal calling by enabling them to answer life's three most important questions:

- Who am I called to be?
- What am I created to do?
- Where am I created to do it?

MORE further unpacks the BE-DO-GO framework and shows the connection between our general calling and our personal calling. It is a useful resource for helping the people in your church discover who God has created them to be and what he has called them to do. To learn more, visit **more-book.com** to download a free *Find Your Calling - Quick Start Guide* and a complete sermon series guide to introduce the idea of personal calling to your church.

Find Your Place: Locating Your Calling Through Gifts, Passions and Story

The GPS personal calling discovery and deployment processed featured in this video will be available through the next book in the Exponential series, *Find Your Place: Locating Your Calling Through Gifts, Passions and Story* by Rob Wegner and Brian Phipps.

RELEASE DATE: March 2019 at The Exponential Conference, Orlando FL.

In addition, a companion kit including:

... a sermon series,
... small group materials,
... an online assessment of GPS with batch reporting of all church members within a congregation,
... an implementation guide for church leaders and
... a 30-minute coaching session with one of the authors will be available via a website and GPS app at the time of the book's release.

For more information now contact **info@disciplesmade.com**.

 IIIADE FOR MORE

ADDITIONAL RESOURCES

ADDITIONAL RESOURCES

Lesson Three: Made to LOVE More: Motivate with Love

Disciples Made:
Disciplesmade.com

This is an entire suite of disciple-making experiences that equip people to be disciples who can make disciples who plant churches that plant churches, built on the foundation of *abiding* and *soul care*.

Followers Made:
This is a six-month experience to discover character and calling, equipping you to be a disciple and make disciples.

Leaders Made:
This is a twelve-month experience to discover servant leadership and what it means to lead a community on mission.

BLESS Learning Community:
This is a six-month experience to develop a lifestyle around five, incarnational rhythms that equip you to live as a missionary where you live, work, study, shop and play.

Simple Church Learning Community:
This is a twelve-month experience that equips you step by step in planting a simple form of church, an extended, spiritual family living on mission together where you live, work, study or play.

Find Your Place:
This is an eight-week launch into discovering and then being deployed into personal calling by triangulating the signals of Gifts, Passions and Story (GPS).

You can visit **disciplesmade.com**. Contact *info@disciplesmade.com* or download the Disciples Made app (available September 2018) to learn more.

Emotionally Healthy Spirituality:
It's Impossible to Be Spiritually Mature, While Remaining Emotionally Immature by Peter Scazzero

Renovation of the Heart: Putting On The Character of Christ by Dallas Willard

ADDITIONAL RESOURCES

Lesson Four: Made to DO More: Organize for Fullness
5Q: Reactivating the Original Intelligence and Capacity of the Body of Christ
by Alan Hirsch

Activating 5Q: A User's Guide
by Alan Hirsch and Jessie Cruickshank

Lesson Five: Made to GO More: Activate with Purpose
The Tangible Kingdom: Creating Incarnational Community
by Hugh Halter and Matt Smay

The Tangible Kingdom Primer: An Eight-Week Guide to Incarnational Community

Lesson Six: Made to WIN More: Prepare for Battle
Freedom Ministries Gateway Church
gatewaypeople.com/ministries/freedom

ADDITIONAL RESOURCES

RELATED MULTIPLICATION RESOURCES

EXPONENTIAL CONFERENCES
Please consider attending one of our Exponential 2019 conferences. Exponential's goal is to help shape your paradigm for multiplication, inspire and encourage you to multiply, and equip you to turn ideas into action.

2019 Theme:
MADE FOR MORE: MOBILIZING GOD'S PEOPLE GOD'S WAY

2019 National Event
March 4 – 7, 2019 | Orlando, FL

Exponential 2019 is our national event, which includes thousands of church multiplication leaders, 150+ Nationally known speakers (including J.D. Greear, Dave Ferguson, Alan Hirsch, Cynthia Marshall and Albert Tate), 200+ Workshops and 15 pre-conference sessions.

2019 Regional Regional Events
Locations and dates:

Washington DC	Chicago, IL
Southern CA	Houston, TX
Bay Area, CA	New York City, NY

Our Exponential regional events are shorter and geographically based (translating to lower overall costs for large teams). Regionals bring the full "punch" of the national conferences' five main stage sessions without the breakout workshops.

For more information, please go to *exponential.org/events*.

FREE EBOOKS
20+ new free eBooks are in our multiplication library. Authors include Brian Sanders, Winfield Bevins, Bill Easum, Todd Wilson, J.D. Greear, Ralph Moore, Larry Walkemeyer, Bruce Wesley, Tim Hawks, Ajai Lall, Brian Bolt, Jeff Leake, and many more. These leaders of multiplying churches share their journey of creating a sending culture of multiplication.

These eBooks are in addition to 60+ existing free eBooks in Exponential's resource library. Check out *exponential.org/ebooks* to download these books.

RESOURCE KIT
Additional Resources

THE BUFORD ONLINE
LIBRARY FOR 100X IMPACT
IN ASSOCIATION WITH MULTIPLIERS

"TRANSFORMING LATENT ENERGY INTO ACTIVE ENERGY FOR KINGDOM IMPACT"

BOB BUFORD: 1939 - 2018

ALMOST THREE DECADES AGO, BOB BUFORD LAUNCHED A MOVEMENT THAT ENABLED 100X KINGDOM RESULTS IN CHURCHES, LEADERS AND MINISTRIES AROUND THE WORLD. IT'S NOW OUR TURN TO CARRY ON WHAT BOB STARTED.

VISIT WWW.BUFORDLIBRARY.ORG TO FIND YOUR PLACE IN THE MOVEMENT.

ADDITIONAL
RESOURCES

ABOUT TODD WILSON

Todd Wilson is co-founder and director of Exponential (exponential. org), a community of activists devoted to church multiplication. The international organization's core focus is distributing resources for church multiplication leaders.

Todd received his B.S. in nuclear engineering from North Carolina State University and a master's degree equivalent from the Bettis Atomic Power Laboratory. For 15 years, he served in the Division of Naval Reactors on nuclear submarine design, operation, maintenance and overhaul.

After a two-year wrestling match with God, Todd entered full-time vocational ministry as the executive pastor at New Life Christian Church where he played a visionary and strategic role for several years as New Life grew and implemented key initiatives such as multisite, externally focused outreach and church planting. His passion for starting healthy new churches continues to grow. Todd now spends most of his energy engaged in a wide range of leading-edge and pioneering initiatives aimed at helping catalyze movements of healthy, multiplying churches.

Todd has written/co-written multiple books, including *Stories of Sifted* (with Eric Reiss), *Spark: Igniting a Culture of Multiplication, Becoming a Level Five Multiplying Church* (with Dave Ferguson), *More: Find Your Personal Calling and Live Life to the Fullest Measure* (Zondervan Publishing), *Dream Big, Plan Smart* (with Will Mancini), *Profiles in Hero Making* (with Dave Ferguson), and *Multipliers*.

Todd is married to Anna and they have two adult sons who are both married — Ben to Therese and Chris to Mariah.

IIIADE FOR MORE

ADDITIONAL RESOURCES

ABOUT ROB WEGNER

Rob Wegner is a Teaching Pastor at Westside Family Church in Kansas City, MO. There, he is helping to advance the Jesus movement both locally and internationally through the development of training pathways, which equips people to live as missionaries where they live, work and play. This movement has promonted and developed simple churches with a network including more than 500 churches in four countries.

Rob is also the Global Catalyst for Relationships and Reproduction for NewThing, a network of more than 1,500 churches in 177 locales. In addition, Rob serves Exponential by leading Learning Communities and speaking at national church conferences. Rob has three books coming out this year. The first is *Find Your Place: Locating Your Calling Through Gifts, Passions and Story* (Zondervan, The More Collective Series, The Exponential Series), which is co-authored with Brian Phipps. *The Starfish and the Church* (Zondervan) is his second book, which he is co-writing with NYT bestselling author Ori Braufman and Lance Ford. His final book this year is the theme book for Exponential 2019, *Made for More: Mobilizing God's People, God's Way*, which he co-wrote with Todd Wilson.

Rob and his wife, Michelle, love living in Kansas City with their three daughters.

ADDITIONAL
RESOURCES

FREE ONLINE MULTIPLICATION ASSESSMENTS
Discover your personal profiles and your church's level and pattern of multiplication via our free online tools. It only takes 20 minutes to complete and is available at becomingfive.org

FREE ONLINE MULTIPLICATION COURSES
The Becoming Five, Dream Big and Hero Maker Courses are designed to delve deeper into the practical elements of church multiplication. Leaders wanting to multiply their church will find valuable training in the form of audio, video, and written content supplied by dozens of multiplying practitioners, with the ability to work at their own pace. Visit *exponential.net* to register.

DIGITAL ACCESS PASSES (TRAINING VIDEOS)
Exponential offers downloadable content from all 10 main stage sessions via our Digital Access Pass (a separate pass for each conference theme) at *exponential.net*.

 2015: "SPARK: Igniting a Culture of Multiplication"

 2016: "Becoming Five"

 2017: "Dream Big: Discover Your Pathway to Level 5 Multiplication"

 2018: "Hero Maker"

 2019: "Made for More: Mobilizing God's People, God's Way"
  -coming in March 2019.

CONNECT WITH EXPONENTIAL:

Twitter - **@churchplanting**

Facebook - **Facebook.com/churchplanting**

Instagram – **church_planting**

IIIADE FOR MORΞ

≡XPONENTIAL⌐

MARCH 4-7, 2019
ORLANDO, FL

TOUR CITIES

WASHINGTON, D.C.
SOUTHERN, CA
BAY AREA, CA
HOUSTON, TX
CHICAGO, IL
NEW YORK, NY

IIIADE FOR MOR≡

SPEAKERS

J.D. GREEAR | OYSTEIN GJERME | ALBERT TATE
DAVE FERGUSON | CYNTHIA MARSHALL | ALAN HIRSCH
DREW HYUN | DAVE CLAYTON | + MORE

FEATURING: TONY DUNGY | LECRAE | + MORE

J.D. GREEAR | CYNTHIA MARSHALL | ALAN HIRSCH | ALBERT TATE

SPECIAL INVITATION
MADE FOR MORE EVENTS

The 2019 Exponential Theme is Made for More: Mobilizing God's People, God's Way. Join us at one of our seven Made for More events starting with our national event in Orlando, Florida. Additional regional events provide opportunities to bring your entire team to an event closer to home.

This book is a taste of our 2019 Made for More theme. Please consider attending one of our seven Exponential 2019 events. Our goal is to help shape your paradigm for multiplication, inspire and encourage you to multiply, and equip you to turn ideas into action. Our 2019 conferences are built on the content of this book and are designed to help you move from ideas and inspiration to implementation and impact.

2019 THEME
MADE FOR MORE:
MOBILIZING GOD'S PEOPLE, GOD'S WAY

2019 NATIONAL MADE FOR MORE EVENT
Exponential // Orlando, Florida // March 4 – 7, 2019

Our national conference, Exponential, is a full-service event in Orlando, Florida with thousands of attendees, 150+ speakers, 40 tracks, 200 workshops and 12+ pre-conference equipping labs.

2019 REGIONAL HEROMAKER EVENTS
**Washington DC, Southern CA, Northern CA, Chicago IL,
Houston TX, and New York City, NY**

Our Exponential regional events are shorter and geographically based which translates to lower overall costs for large teams. Regionals bring the full "punch" of the national conferences' five main stage sessions without the breakout workshops.

www.exponential.org/events

IIIADE FOR MOR≡